M000313603

Souled Out

Souled Out

Inspirational Stories on Beating the Odds
with Radical Faith & Prayer

CHERYL POLOTE-WILLIAMSON

purposely
created
PUBLISHING

Special discounts are available on bulk quantity purchases by book clubs, associations and special interest groups. For details email:
sales@publishyourgift.com
or call (888) 949-6228.

For information logon to:
www.PublishYourGift.com

This book is dedicated to my dear friend and Link sister Karla Fuller. Words cannot express the beauty that Karla brought into the lives of everyone who came in contact with her. My heart is full knowing that Karla's words and her story will endure forever on the pages of *Souled Out*. Rest in heaven, Karla.

We love you.

A portion of the proceeds from this book will go to fighting ovarian cancer.

Table of Contents

Acknowledgments

My Whys (The reasons why I do what I do):
Russell Jr., Lauren, Courtney, and Leah

My Dream Team:
Pamela Eno, Rhonda Jones, and Shani McIlwain

Tieshena Davis & Purposely Created Publishing Group

My Best Friend & Life Partner: My husband, Russ

Three Strikes You're In: My Journey with Ovarian Cancer and God

KARLA FULLER

"I can do all things through Christ who strengthens me."

Philippians 4:13 (NKJV)

My purpose for writing this chapter is to encourage others who are going through cancer or other life adversities. I want to let you know that anything is possible through prayer, faith, and Jesus Christ. God has a plan for us even in our adversity.

My cancer journey began in 2010. I was six years into my happy marriage, going to Zumba class weekly, working, and immersed in church, my profession, and women's organizations. Life was good until strike one.

One day, I noticed that my abdomen felt hard. I had a previously scheduled appointment on a Friday with my nephrologist, who is my guardian angel. I decided I would ask him about it then. He examined me and said that my stomach felt hard, I looked girthier than usual, and asked, "How long has this been going on?" I answered, "About a month." He responded, "Why didn't you tell me sooner?" I answered that I knew I was going to see him soon. He left the examination room. I could hear him behind the door talking to my internist on the phone. He returned with a concerned look and said, "Please go see your internist on Monday." That Monday, I saw my internist. She shared that I had a large mass in my abdomen, and I would have to have a hysterectomy. She referred me to an oncologist, who saw me right away. I felt an instant connection with this doctor. During the consultation, he stated that he was going to perform surgery on Friday. I almost fell out of my chair because I was thinking we would probably go to surgery within the month. He reminded me that I was in an oncologist's office and that's how it works. I also immediately connected with the oncologist's nurse. It's amazing how God puts the right people in your life at the right time. I notified my boss, who is a Christian, and he was totally supportive. We set a plan in place for other attorneys to cover for me during my surgery and recovery. During this process, I had no fear because I knew God was with me. I regularly prayed for healing.

About a month after surgery, I learned that I had a bowel obstruction. However, I knew that God was with me. Shortly thereafter, I had bowel obstruction removal surgery. Unfortunately, the bowel obstruction surgery was not successful, and I was told I would need to have a second bowel obstruction surgery within a month. Three surgeries in one year!

I was in the hospital recovering for two months (which is unheard of these days, but all things are possible through Christ), and God allowed me to have so many angels in my life. My husband has been my rock and best friend throughout this process. He stayed positive and encouraging, visiting every day and spending many nights with me in the hospital.

Being an only child, I am incredibly blessed to have married into a family that is genuine and caring. My sisters-in-law and brothers-in-law cooked food, visited regularly, brought flowers, and did all the things that Christian families do. My Aunt Betty, who has been like a mother to me since my mother died, came from Maryland for each of the surgeries. She's a guardian angel too. She charmed my doctors with her wit, self-help books, and life advice. My cousins and stepchildren called and checked on me, and my best friends called constantly giving me much needed support. The comfort and care ministry at Oak Cliff Bible Fellowship was awesome! Someone from the church visited every week, brought little gifts, and I received cards from church members that I did not even know. It was heartwarming to know that my church home practices what it preaches. The flow of cards from family, friends, and associates was an overwhelming display of love.

Tip #1: Having a Christian support network is critical when going through adversity!

Also, my women's groups and coworkers were very supportive, with many members and employees visiting. The hospital staff was also great! The head nurse allowed me to have one of the larger rooms that had a desk where I could work. God allowed so much love to flow during this time, and He worked through many angels. Once I recovered from the surgeries, I went through five rounds of chemotherapy, and hair loss. Through prayer and God's grace, I worked the entire time.

Tip #2: Prayer and a spirit of gratitude is key to God's grace.

My wonderful hair stylist, a Christian friend, went wig shopping with me and picked out a wig close to my hair color that she cut and styled.

Tip #3: My philosophy is, you may be sick, but you do not have to look sick.

Keep your hair, makeup, and clothes looking top notch! My oncologist and God allowed me to go on a long-planned trip with my husband and close friends to Europe and a women's organization convention. Next came the scans and the waiting game. Each year without cancer was a blessing from God and a milestone. I was living and enjoying life. I made it to my fifth year cancer free! It was a bittersweet time when my oncologist released me from his care around August 2015, as I had a special bond with him and his nurse.

And then, strike two.

Fast forward to September 2015. I am in my nephrologist's office again for a routine check-up. He performs a routine blood test and tells me my creatinine levels are high. He recommends that I drink more water. For the next few months, I drink water like there is no tomorrow. I return for a follow-up visit around December, repeat the test, and the creatinine level is still high. Thus, he decided to perform further testing. He ordered a sonogram that revealed a blockage around my kidney. Afterward, he advised me to return to my oncologist. The oncologist said that if he were a betting man, he would bet that the cancer had returned. This was disheartening, but I knew that if God brought me through it once, He would bring me through it again.

Tip #4: Always trust God! A CT scan confirmed this blockage.

The cancer had returned and attached itself to one of my kidneys. This time, the surgery was going to require my oncologist to remove the cancer, a colorectal surgeon to clear the bowel, and a kidney surgeon to remove the affected kidney. As I sat in the kidney surgeon's office, I cringed to hear the words that one kidney needed to be removed. My oncologist had the same recommendation because if left, it could potentially spread cancer elsewhere in my body. I really had to wrap my brain around that. On the other hand, God has blessed us with two kidneys, and we only need one to function.

Tip #5: Stay positive!

Again, I faced my boss and told him the bad news. He was totally supportive and gave me a rubber armband that said, "God is Big Enough." I wore it for encouragement. Sometimes it's just the little things that God does to cheer us up. In February 2016, my aunt returned for my surgery and was a huge help afterward. It was very comforting when an elder from church came and prayed with me prior to my surgery. The surgery was a success, and the recovery time was six to eight weeks. Again, attorneys filled in for me during my absence, and my cousin from Atlanta came and stayed in the hospital with me for a week to keep me company. My best friends called, and my husband was always there—steady and full of faith. My coworkers, friends, and family sent gifts, called, and texted. God always showers you with angels, just trust Him. Many of my friends, relatives, and in-laws prayed prayers of faith, and I did too. I never questioned God about why the cancer came back. We may not understand, but I know that everything that happens is a part of His divine plan. I made it through six rounds of chemotherapy, and worked through it all trusting in Jesus. I was trusting God for another five years of being cancer free and then, strike three.

Around January 2017, I felt a pain in my abdomen (a new symptom). I dismissed it as nothing to worry about; but, by February 2017, I was having frequent little pinprick pains. This sent me back to my oncologist's office. Before he announced it, I knew it was cancer. I did not question God. I trusted God to get me through this ordeal again according to His will and purpose.

Our first attempt was to test my previous cancer sample to see if it was estrogen sensitive and if I could take a medicine called tamoxifen. The sample came back negative, so that was not an option. We could not do a biopsy because of where the cancer was situated and because it would be too dangerous. My oncologist advised that I should receive more chemotherapy, but a different type. Because it was so soon after the previous surgery, another surgery was out of the question.

I thought about getting a second opinion at one of the top medical centers in Houston. I prayed to God to let me share this with my oncologist diplomatically, because I respect him very much. As God would have it, after my oncologist explained my options, he stated that I might want to get a second opinion. God opened the door! I then shared that I wanted a second opinion at the medical center in Houston and asked my oncologist if he had a contact. He provided the name of an oncologist there, and made the initial contact. God is good!

My husband and I drove to Houston to meet with the referred oncologist. We stayed at a familiar suite hotel chain and received a fairly good rate on short notice. When we arrived, the receptionist hesitated as she looked for our reservation. I became irritated and was just about to say something. But, sometimes you need to keep your mouth shut! At that moment, she informed us that she found a lower rate because we were going to the medical center. God steps in right when you need Him. I became very friendly with this receptionist (who I almost told off!) over the course of my stay.

The referred oncologist offered three options: chemo-therapy, clinical trial, or radiation. He advised that radiation was the best option for a possible cure, although it would have potential risks due to my bowel issues. He further advised that I speak with a radiation oncologist, a female doctor who he described as one of the best in the world. The oncologist stated that I could have chemotherapy anywhere, but radiation is like an art, and he highly recommended that I have it in Houston where he claimed they had the best radiation technologists in the world. Before we left Houston, I signed an agreement to have six weeks of radiation treatment. I was permitted to telework from my hotel room the entire time we were there. I worked harder and longer in that hotel room than I did while in my office in Arlington. I think there is something about solitary, uninterrupted time. The hotel we stayed in the first time we traveled to Houston included many amenities, however, it did not include a com-plimentary shuttle to the medical center like many of the other hotels. Therefore, I started checking with other hotels (that were more expensive), and my husband suggested that I check again with our original hotel. I did, and we received an even better rate because I was not going to check out on the weekends. Also, by the time I called back, they had a complimentary shuttle to the medical center! God worked it all out! All things are possible through Christ!

Week one of treatment went well! The technicians were awesome! They played my favorite jazz tunes during treatments. On Friday of the first week, I received two urgent messages from the medical center's financial con-sultant stating that she needed to speak with me about my insurance. I had an uneasy feeling. When I reported for treatment on Monday, she informed me that my insurance denied coverage as medically unnecessary. She assured me that she and my doctor were going to battle to appeal the decision, and they felt confident that it would be overturned on appeal. This was a downer for me, and I asked whether I should go home and stop treatment until it was appealed successfully. The consultant told me that under no circumstances was I to stop treatment and that she did not want me to worry about anything except getting well. I prayed, "Lord, I know that You did not bring me this far and work everything out perfectly to leave me."

Tip #6: At your lowest point, look up and pray!

I did not even want to think about the exorbitant cost of this treatment, which in my mind would be hundreds of thousands of dollars. I trusted in God, had faith, prayed, and requested the prayers of my women's prayer group. One of the ladies in my morning prayer group worked for my insurance company and stated that she was praying fervently that her company would not let me down. Through God's grace, the coverage was upheld on appeal!

As I continued with my treatment, there was an encouraging sisterhood among the women in the dressing room before treatment. Everyone had a story and we encouraged each other.

Tip #7: When you are going through, God will place others in your life for you to minister to.

It's important to encourage others as you are going through! It helps them and you.

There were women of all ages, races, and nationalities from all over the world, including Qatar, Israel, Mexico, and other parts of the United States, receiving cancer treatments. As we all completed our treatment, we went through the tradition of ringing a bell three times. Following treatments, the doctors told me that they wanted me to receive chemotherapy, a fact not revealed prior to radiation. So, as I write this chapter, I am currently going through chemotherapy. I will experience hair loss, but I know God is with me throughout this journey. I will survive and thrive. I now have more of an urgency about my life goals because this is my third strike. I am in God's game whether that means more time on Earth or in eternity. Either way, I win, and you will too!

Face What's Facing You!
When Facing Unknowns...Trust, Rise, or Collapse?

DR. RENEE FOWLER HORNBUCKLE

*"Your destiny shall NOT die, you were born with a purpose
and there is an expected end for your life."*

Dr. Renee Fowler Hornbuckle

*"What's more, I am with you, and will protect you wherever you
go, and will bring you back safely to this land; I will be with you
constantly until I have finished giving you all I am promising."*

Genesis 28:15 (TLB)

Not long ago, I was living my life believing the best of times had arrived. According to society's standards, my family and those who were connected to us were all living the "American Dream." Everything was great. Everything pointed to success. We had risen to the top by the world's standards and by how I believed God wanted us to be blessed!

Because life had been so good and I was enjoying such wonderful success, I (like others) ignored what you would call signs and indicators of pending danger. I must admit that even as a person of strong faith, I really had not paid much attention to the Bible Scriptures that forewarned me to be on the lookout for unexpected challenges. That's how life often is; things are going along well and then something happens that steals our hope and robs us of joy. It just seems that trouble is often lurking around the corner waiting to attack. And attack it did.

Little did I know that at the end of 2005 we were going to be confronted by insurmountable difficulties in a host of unimaginable ways. I would never have thought that my life as I knew it, and every dream that I had and was living, would not only be challenged, but would appear to be shattered beyond repair, literally laying in pieces.

During the best of times, I found myself unprepared for the worst of times that were lurking just around the corner. Like many people, I assumed that because I was successful and blessed, I had nothing to worry about. I believed that life could only get better! Then, the most difficult challenge I would ever face came storming in disguised as a crisis, bringing with it shock, disbelief, discouragement, and pain. The crisis further presented itself with all the components of public scandal, embarrassment, humiliation, pain, heartbreak, doubt, domestic abuse, silent suffering, loss of finances, loss of possessions, and betrayal! In the natural, you would think that a person could not possibly withstand all of this at one time, but somehow God allowed me to be able to bear it all.

Now, having come through these difficulties by the grace of God, I can clearly see His process that prepared me to face and overcome the greatest challenges of my life. As I sought God to make sense of it all, I realized I just had to accept that: 1) God is real. He loved me and still had a plan for my life, 2) My challenges were real. I could face them with God's help and power and rise or I could succumb to them. Have you ever felt this way or had experiences and circumstances that caused you to question life and God? Have you ever asked the question, "How much more do I have to go through?" Have you ever told God, "I can't take any more!"? These are the exact conversations I had with God while facing personal, relational, financial, and professional loss. The one thing that I was thankful for was that I didn't lose my mind! I needed to be able to think and process clearly. I needed to hear God with clarity and maneuver through the loss caused not by anything I created, but by being connected to someone (my ex) who made selfish choices that inflicted pain, suffering, and produced an environment that made it difficult for me to recover for years.

To be able to focus in tough times, you must get clarity. When you can think right, you can assess right, and get a clear plan of what you need to do. As unimaginable challenges were confronting me on every side, I took a realistic assessment of my personal belief system. I had to look at my faith, my strength, and my beliefs. I had to get clarity, or even perhaps a new view on life, so that I could do more than just cope. Simply tolerating or coping with my pain wasn't an option. My life touched the lives of too many others (most importantly, those of my children and our congregation) to be overcome by opposition. I had to courageously confront, identify, and deal with the mounting difficulties we faced as effectively as possible, so that with the help of God I could create a strategy to eliminate and overcome this calamity in my life.

It would have been easy for me to become angry, to quit, or to give up; but, God would not allow me to be bitter nor to quit. Instead, I faced what was facing me. I confronted my troubles rather than collapsing into them. Instead of asking, "God, why did you allow this to happen?" I simply reached deep into my soul and asked, "How can this be used for any good?"

It's not necessarily wrong to ask why, but it's better to ask, how can this be used for good and what can be learned? We must open our eyes and look deeper. Could it be that you had to go through this so that your true purpose would be revealed? This is difficult for people to grasp. Honestly, I don't fully comprehend why bad things happen, but I choose to believe that what doesn't kill me can make me wiser, stronger, and available to be both help and hope to someone. If you recognize that God is equipping you to rise above the power of your pain amid your greatest crisis, you can begin to take your life back.

My life is a testimony of God's transforming and restorative power. I transformed into a stronger and wiser individual despite what I experienced through our very tragic family crisis. I did so by developing a level of discipline, focus, and confidence in my new identity. It was important that I recognize that I could rise above the negative circumstances. I asked God how He intended to use this for good because my children, my family and friends, my church, and my community were depending on me. I believe that He wanted me to be a living example of hope to others. My pain caused me to be transformed for a greater purpose—giving hope to the hopeless. Teaching others how to overcome and manage crisis is a weighty yet noble assignment, and I told God I would step up to the challenge.

So, are you facing the unknowns in life because of dire circumstances or poor choices? First, accept that through your pain, challenge, or trouble, God can and is prompting positive change in you and developing you for greater. I have found that difficulties have a tremendous power to change you and make you better equipped to handle life. Keep in mind: 1) You can change for better or for worse, 2) You can get stronger or weaker, 3) You can become more positive or more negative, 4) You can become more hopeful or more cynical; the choice is yours.

Realistically, I realize that embracing anything or making a choice in the middle of a painful challenge is difficult; but, we must do so or we will develop coping mechanisms or beliefs that are not beneficial to our positive progress. You must recognize that your destiny is at stake here. Remember, regardless of what happened in our lives, we are each trying to reach an expected outcome that God has waiting for us. So, things that hinder you, like unforgiveness or negative coping mechanisms, must be removed. Negative coping mechanisms often include: 1) Running away (taking flight) from our problems, 2) Hiding from our problems or hoping our problems will magically disappear so that we can avoid dealing with them, 3) Succumbing to a temporary fix (this can include over-shopping, over-eating, over-cleaning, etc., and range from occasional use of over-the-counter drugs to alcohol and/or drug abuse), and finally 4) Taking out our pain and disappointment on others (kick the dog mentality). These things become hindrances to our healing and recovery.

If we don't own our truth and embrace the difficulty, we will never fully recover. If you embrace it, deal with it, and learn to respond in the right manner, you can overcome no matter what has happened in your life! (1 John 5:4)

Yes, I agree that when calamity occurs, it can be difficult to locate "the good." Locating "the good" requires you to take charge of your life. As I faced what was facing me, I had to trust the Lord and continue making the right choices for a good result. While overwhelming, to bring about a renewed life (in my case, re-engaging in life after a horrific scandal) I had to embrace the challenge. Embracing the challenge is a required part of the process toward things turning for the better.

Next, you must gain the confidence to face where you are, take charge of your situation (your life), and respond as needed to get you to the place God has for you! You are more resilient than you know. You can overcome where you are and reach the good that awaits. It's important to note that with every life challenge, test, and difficulty anyone can learn, heal, grow, and mature. The choice is yours!

I chose to believe that God had a plan for me and that He would help me face each situation with grace, strength, and dignity. It's human nature to desire a perfect life, for things to be "just right," but we must realize that troubles and challenges will come, and they usually arrive at inconvenient times. It is these "interruptions" that test our faith in God and challenge our perspective.

Through my personal experiences, I learned to trust and believe more in God. Rather than focusing on my horrific, scandalous circumstances, believing completely in God taught me to focus on increasing my level of faith so that I could identify the actual lesson that was to be learned and the strength to be gained. Most importantly, I learned to trust in the fact that no matter the circumstances, God would pull me through! I guess you could say I was Souled Out! And you know what, God came through each time!

When life falls apart and you don't know what's next or how to recover, it can be unbearable. Facing the unknown or the unforeseeable requires an elevated level of faith. But by trusting in God, who knows your situation, eventually the unknown becomes known.

God has guided me through every step of my public scandal and struggles. He's the One (with the help of trusted counsel) who has brought me to the place of restoration. It hasn't always been easy (yes, I cried many nights), but my faith and hope in God kicked in and gave me renewed strength!

Strong faith in God gave me the confidence to re-engage in life after public scandal, embarrassment, humiliation, pain, heartbreak, domestic abuse, silent suffering, loss of finances and possessions, and betrayal. Strong faith healed me, strengthened me, gave me the hope to believe again, and the confidence to face my unknowns and rise to an even greater life!

The truth is we have all faced disappointments and difficulties in life. Each of us can look back and reflect on negative or disappointing experiences. Many things can go wrong; we can find ourselves in places that are far from where we originally felt we should be. We all know that life does not always turn out as we planned. This is an indisputable fact. Nevertheless, God has promised that if we trust Him and stand on His promises, we will be victorious (Isaiah 40:28-31). I learned to stand, wait upon the lord, and endure spiritually, mentally, emotionally, intellectually, and in any other way you can imagine. To endure means to withstand; and, like I did, you can withstand the pressure, the stress, and the weight of whatever comes your way. You must face what is before you. The quicker you face it, the quicker you can move on. Once you face your challenge, you can begin to make a turn for the better and pick up the pieces of your life, your business, and your world.

> Humpty Dumpty sat on a wall,
> Humpty Dumpty had a great fall;
> All the king's horses, and all the king's men
> Couldn't put Humpty together again.

After hearing this simple nursery rhyme, most of us live thinking that our lives will never be put back together again. That is the farthest from the truth!

Remember, it's how you react to the things that are going on around you that determines how the pieces are picked up. Your life can be put back together again, if you are willing to work through the process. Through the broken pieces and challenges, you can rise and enjoy the life God desires for you!

P – Pray
I   – Imagine yourself in a better place
E – Endure the pain to bring about the change
C – Commit to the change
E – Execute a new life plan
S – Soar into the new life that awaits you

The Evolution of Perseverance

ROBERT FAULK

*"For ye have need of patience, that, after ye have done
the will of God, ye might receive the promise."*

Hebrews 10:36 (KJV)

In a world where instant popcorn, microwave dinners and two-minute drive through food venues are the norm, I am amazed that God's timetable is not moved by the limitation of time. In 1997, I answered the call to pastor. Not knowing how this assignment would unfold, I began the process of preparing a people to impact their faith, family, and finances. I was determined to give this opportunity my all.

When one starts a new opportunity, the challenge is energizing and fresh. However, when the reality of obstacles and challenges set in, you must evaluate your ability to persevere when what you heard and see differ. In this journey, I will share with you how I evolved into a person who understands that time is your friend and not a debilitating foe. I want my experience to become the foundation for which anyone can realize their destiny through perseverance. Perseverance is defined in Webster's dictionary as: a continued effort to do or achieve something despite difficulties, failure, or opposition. This definition speaks to the heart of the process I endured and that you will have to walk through to achieve your dreams and life goals. For me, the dream and goals are one and the same—to finish my God-given assignment.

As I mentioned, God's assignment for me was to pastor. However, I did not fully understand what this opportunity would entail. For you to fully understand the depth of my journey, I have to take you back to an event that shaped the moment. In 1990, I was a member of a progressive and thriving church. Our church was experiencing outstanding growth. All facets of the church were growing; the nursery, children's church, and the main sanctuary were packed. We had to start another service on Sunday morning and launch a Spanish service at 5:00 p.m. Because of the tremendous growth, we needed to increase our pastoral staff. Therefore, I was ordained as an associate pastor in 1994.

My ordination was the foundation of all the spiritual steps, and the outline to the goals that I would begin to take toward this journey of perseverance. It was during that ordination service that God laid out the skeleton of His plan for my life. With this plan, I began to prepare my family to embrace the possibility that God had presented to me. My vision was to start an inner-city word of faith church that would embrace all of God's people while focusing on the down-trodden, broken, and hurt—those who had all but given up on life and the thought of God. With vision in my heart, I continued to serve faithfully in that church.

In 1996, during a fellowship dinner at my pastor's house, he asked his associate pastors if they felt called to pastor their own church. Out of the several pastors we had on staff, another pastor and I said that we thought God had called us to shepherd a church congregation. Thinking back to that moment, I now realize that my saying yes in the natural opened the door to a spiritual assignment.

Several months later, during our annual church fellowship conference, I received a confirming word that God wanted me to launch this inner-city word of faith church. Excited, yet unsure about my destiny, I wanted to talk to my pastor for guidance and advice; so, my wife and I scheduled a meeting with him. After I explained the vision and plans to my pastor, his words were reserved and somewhat limited. He wanted to know what motivated me to make that determination. Then, he cut right to the heart of his evaluation and told me that I should start my pursuit now and leave immediately. My wife and I left that meeting uncertain about the next steps.

Still seeking God for guidance and clarity, my wife and I went to church the Sunday following that meeting. As we entered the sanctuary and sat down in the back, my pastor's wife was starting the morning announcements. She began to recap a meeting that they had with a man who stated he was a pastor and who deceived them with untruths. She went on to say that this man could not be trusted, and he needed to leave. Hurting in the pew but unable to say or express any words, I sat there in the service knowing that I was the subject of the announcement. I was exiled with no church to go to and no pastor to cover the church God wanted me to shepherd.

Fighting through the pain of being rejected and misrepresented, I began to pursue the mandate and calling on my life. When you are called by God, there is a drive and a determination that will not allow you to throw in the towel and quit. The opportunities God gives will often be wrapped as a problem or a challenging situation. Yet, I saw it as an excellent chance to see God work on my behalf.

When God gives us an assignment, He only gives us enough information to get started. The start of any endeavor is the big picture; the overall objective or strategy—the five, ten, or fifteen-year plan. The individual goals and specific tasks of this plan must be sought out through prayer and seeking God. When you seek the face of God, don't just inquire about what is in His hand but seek Him for who He is. You position yourself to experience the best of God when you are interested in the fine details of the plan. You can trust God's plan because He only wants the best for you (Jeremiah 29:11).

The plan that God assigned to me was simple, "To increase His family with people, transformed by His word, showing compassion to His Body and outreach to the world, as we glorify God through worship." Those five components were the framework for executing the plan and assignment on my life.

With great anticipation, excitement, and joy, the church and assignment were born. Prior to the launching of the church, I still had to solve the dilemma of not having a pastor or covering. Not knowing how or who God would use to solve this critical problem, I consulted friends, loved ones, and peers for possible answers. As I sought the Lord, a trusted friend and spiritual brother, Reggie Williams, introduced me to the man who would become my spiritual father and pastor. In October 1996, I sat down with Bishop Sam Drye, whom the Lord used to establish the insight I needed to be reenergized and motivated to continue pursuing the call and assignment on my life.

After that meeting, I re-embraced my assignment and my family, and I celebrated the New Year of 1997 in our home. This was the first time in years that I was not physically in a church building celebrating the start of a new calendar year. The feelings and thoughts I experienced were strange because I had no church connection or sense of belonging. This place I was in was unfamiliar. I was alone, but not by myself. I was starting over; yet, deep within me I knew that this place was not it. God was not going to leave me here. I held on to the Scripture in 2 Corinthians 4:8-9 (NJKV): "We are hard-pressed on every side, yet not crushed; we are perplexed, but not in despair; persecuted, but not forsaken; struck down, but not destroyed." It is this hope and perseverance that kept me going. The same should keep you going.

Perseverance should not be just a nice saying or buzz word to use as a motto. It must be a determination that, when properly executed, yields you the strength needed to continue in the face of opposition. When you persevere, you don't quit. You may not have all the answers, but you don't quit. People you counted on may have left, but you don't quit. All the money you require may not show up when needed, but you don't quit. To quit an assignment that God called you to is to say that He made a mistake. Romans 11:29 states that the gifts and talents God bestowed upon us and the calling He has for you to fulfill were not a fluke nor happenstance but a divine mandate. He knew what you were capable of before you were physically placed into existence or manifested in this earthly realm. Your purpose is a divine answer to the problems that exist in this world. You possess all the necessary tools and skills to do whatever God has called you to produce. God is not like mankind whom He created. He cannot lie. Nor did God come from mankind that He should repent. What He said He will do, and when He speaks it shall come to pass (Numbers 23:19).

God did exactly what He said He was going to do in my life. In January 1997, the vision of becoming a church began. I will never forget that first Tuesday at the then Ramada Inn. Wow! It seems like yesterday. With my family and one or two other people, Faith Tabernacle World Outreach Center's Bible Study was officially launched. Though we were small in number, I taught as if there were hundreds of people present. God is a faithful God. He made good on His promise to me. The dream of an inner-city word of faith church was now a reality.

Everything I had endured resulted in a victory because I was willing to pay the price of perseverance. I realized that I was able to withstand the devastating blows of rejection and misunderstanding. I was able to hold fast to the plan and vision God gave me; a vision that included the good, the bad, and the ugly. When you are in hot pursuit of the call of God, you must understand the attacks and demonic distractions that will come. Satan, to discredit God, will always try to keep you from accomplishing what God wants to do in your life. But God brings you out and into your destiny when you persevere.

From that very impactful moment, I learned the following lessons during my evolution of perseverance. First, I understood that God was preparing my ability to stand and not falter. By allowing me to go through that situation, I had to learn to overcome by fortifying my resolve in what I heard God say. When you hear God's plan, it is always in the future tense with a now implication. God speaks to you with a completed action. His announcement is to put you on notice. The notice of information alerts you that it is time to start. Then, God only gives you additional information on a need to know basis. Once you get started, it is your job to finish.

Secondly, I realized that God equipped me with the ability to accomplish His calling on my life. As I mentioned previously, His call is more than being summoned—it is the empowerment God gives you to achieve anything. Paul had it right when he declared that he could do all things through Christ that gave him the strength. Your abilities will only be recognized and fully understood when you are tested and challenged. The ordeal I experienced was hurtful but necessary. I became a better more motivated servant and child of God. I learned to trust God's instruction and information, no matter how much or little He reveals.

Lastly, I learned that quitting was never the option I would embrace. The fact that God called me to serve in the kingdom was not only a calling but a mandate. Like my Savior, Jesus Christ, I realized that this was a privilege and not a right; therefore, who was I to put my hand to the plow and take it back? God had equipped me, and I could do it. God is obligated to finish what He started, and because we have His DNA we can finish what we start.

These lessons helped to develop my perseverance, which solidified my being Souled Out to God. The reason you can develop perseverance is because God chose you. From the foundation of the earth, God chose your beginning from your end. He ordained you to establish your purpose and reason for existence. He's counting on you to do your part in establishing His kingdom by yielding yourself as an extension of His hand. You are equipped and graced with what is needed to face any trial or challenge that you encounter. God has invested much in you and you are required to give Him dividends.

He is in expectation of reaping those dividends, but you must be prepared for the obstacles that will come. Obstacles you must anticipate overcoming could present themselves as: self-sabotage, societal or cultural influences, and Satan's strategies. In self-sabotage, we tend to talk ourselves out of what God has said about us. We use our fears, family, and our failures to justify why we can't accomplish the thing God has called us to perform. For example, when Moses was called to save Israel, he complained that he had difficulty speaking clearly; so, God added Aaron to make up his deficiency. At the end of Moses' destiny, he did exactly what God said. As you are reading this, cease from self-sabotage. Societal and cultural influences often undermine the potential a called individual has by telling you things such as: "This hasn't been done before," "Others have attempted your idea and experienced failure," or "You, like Jesus, are measured by your family background." The latter is like David when the prophet Nathan was looking for the next king. Upon arriving at Jesse's house, he figured one of the son's he saw would be king. But, the one that was called had not yet arrived. The Scripture says that man looks on the outward, but God knows the heart (1 Samuel 16:7). Lastly, Satan devises all kinds of plans to try to obstruct you, but because we are not ignorant we see his devices. Therefore, when you are challenged your remedy is very simple: Submit to God, resist the opposition or obstacle, and it will flee (James 4:7).

After taking a short glimpse of my journey and how I learned to persevere through the thing I had to suffer, my prayer is that you now have a foundation you can use to assist you in your journey. I need to remind you once again that God does not make mistakes. He is a sovereign God who is worthy of our trust and service. God has a great plan for you. Your perseverance allows you to see your journey through to the end.

A New Thing

SHANI MCILWAIN

"Whoever is a believer in Christ is a new creation. The old way of living has disappeared. A new way of living has come into existence."

2 Corinthians 5:17 (GW)

I was seated in a central cellblock waiting for my finger-prints to come back from a national database that confirmed I did not have any additional warrants. I was the former Girl Scout, the former scholarship winner, the former youth group leader. I had been afforded a great childhood filled with love, values, character, faith, and structure. As my first 24 years of my life flashed before my eyes, I realized that I had taken this wrong turn, and honestly I did not even know how I ended up here in this position. I believed in God, yet I was working for the devil. I didn't even realize it at the time, but nearly 20 years later the generational curse that followed and plagued my father would now cause me strife.

It all started when I got my first "real job" working for the federal government. Almost instantly, I was surrounded by people who loved to spend money and spend lots of it. I was a single parent starting at the bottom of the pay scale, just barely making ends meet. I made too much money for assistance and not enough money to live on my own. Every month there was a deficit. One day, I was three weeks behind on my daycare bill. When I went to the daycare, the owner (a pastor), told me to go get the money and leave my son with her. It was the most humiliating feeling ever. I felt she was holding my child ransom for $300. I compromised my morals and standards to get the money for that bill by reaching out to an old "friend" (or sex partner, I should say). That was not my best moment at all. I was in such a dark place. Every day at work I would sit with these women who spent their lunch breaks at the most expensive mall in the city. It was nothing for them to just pull out a credit card and spend $500. One of my friends at the time, April, was also a single mother. She explained to me how she managed to drive a nice car, have two daughters in private school, and buy a house. I really needed to understand what I was doing wrong, and how I could get to her level. She had a "friend" she would spend time with who performed certain acts on her, or vice versa, for a small fee. She continued to tell me that her "friend" always had friends looking for someone like her.

After months of saying no, I reluctantly said yes when I got the cut off notice for my electricity and a court paper for rent. On a sunny Saturday afternoon, I met my friend at her house, and we rode together to Malcolm's office. When we arrived, there was wine and food waiting for us just like she said. Malcolm was so excited to see April. They greeted each other in a loving and affectionate way. My setup was sitting on the couch like he was mad. His vibe was all off, and

I was already a bit nervous so that was not helping. As my friend departed the main room and handled her business, I sat awkwardly wishing I had never agreed to have sex for money. I guess God has a way of blocking things He knows you are not ready for just to protect you.

As the silence continued, I finally broke the ice by saying, "So, April tells me you love Kendall Jackson wine." He said, "No, not really." What? I am staring at three bottles of Kendall Jackson wine in the ice bucket. I went back to silence. So, he then began to ask me if I worked, how many kids I had, and where I was from. Basic questions people ask before they go in for the "big ask," I suppose. I answered them as quickly as I could, giving one-word answers when I could. Then, as the wine was beginning to loosen my inhibitions this fool said, "I thought you were going to be a little thinner." I replied, "I thought you were going to be a little younger." My life as a prostitute ended before it began; however, my money woes did not.

I continued to struggle. I would go to organizations seeking help only to be turned down repeatedly because $11.79 an hour was considered to be too much income. I could not seem to get out of the hole. One day, I was approached by someone at work to pay a fake claim. I could get a kick back. The probability of getting caught was almost none. I did it. My first payout was $700. A few days later, I did it again. This time I received $2,000. I paid all my bills. I was hooked. It was like a drug. For months, I had stopped eating out with my coworkers or going out with them during lunch. Right after my first payment, I went out with them and bought a Coach wallet. I felt like I had experienced some financial freedom. Who knew that this false sense of freedom would eventually cost me my soul?

I spent the next 18 months making false claims and paying them. I helped anyone that needed help. I paid off debts for friends and took care of family. You could say I was the modern-day Robin Hood. But I knew it was not right. I knew that eventually I would get caught, yet I also knew that the easiest way to get caught was to tell someone, so I did not tell a soul. I kept this secret hidden away from everyone. At night, I would pray to God asking Him to help me stop. It was addictive. Sometimes, I would just do it because I could. I was no longer doing it out of need or desperation; I would do it because I was good at it. Then, guilt would swoop in and I would go to church and put it in the collection plate. It was the craziest life ever. I would literally sit at my desk fighting to not do wrong. I started to bring a Bible to work with me thinking that it would help. But the Bible works when you open it, not just when you sit it on a desk. How naïve was I to think that God is so mystical and magical that He can "poof" and allow me to stop stealing? I was a thief plain and simple, and I was about to get caught. I was caught over a math error of five dollars. Five dollars! When I was confronted at my desk to show documentation, I was so valued and respected that they did not even think anything negative. I said I was on my way to lunch and they said, "No problem, Shani, just bring it when you get back from lunch." I never went back.

A week later, an investigator called and asked me to come to his office to discuss the situation. I hung up on him, and then blocked his number. I called a lawyer in the phone book and was told that his retainer was $10,000. He gave me some free advice, but the one thing I remember was that he prayed with me. Two years would go by before I had to fully confront this incident. I had gone on to get another job, and tried to live a life that was not filled with lies and deceit. Then I received a letter to appear at the U.S. Attorney's Office. It was time to face my past.

The case took another two years to get resolved. I went through two public defenders who seemed to not have my best interest at heart. As a result, when the case got transferred it took five months to get a new attorney assigned to me. The second one was very compassionate and thorough. I read every case file similar to mine that she gave me. During one meeting, she said I should have become a lawyer because I would have made a great one.

During the time of my legal problems, my mother was battling cancer. I was so embarrassed and ashamed to even bring this to her. I decided not to fight the charges. I was going to plead guilty, and fight for a lighter sentence. I couldn't put my mother through a trial. It took almost seven months for my sentencing hearing. I was facing three to nine years. I had never been in trouble a day in my life. Who was going to take care of my children and my mother?

I spent many, many nights praying and crying, crying and praying. I had to write a letter to the judge regarding why I should be given the minimum sentence. I had so many people around me saying I should focus on not having a father in my life. While that is true, it was not the reason I stole money. I stole money because I lost hope. I stole money because I was greedy and selfish. I had made a choice. The choices we make in life can either negatively or positively affect us. I wasn't thinking about my children when I stole over $100,000. That is the amount that was on all the court documents.

Over a two-year period, I had produced false claims and committed wire fraud. Blaming my father, a man I had never met, seemed like the easy thing to do, but it also seemed like I was minimizing the role that my mother had in my life or the role my grandparents played. I had a good childhood. They instilled in me a value system that should not have allowed me to do what I did. I could not and did not blame my lack of a father.

On the day of sentencing, I went to court by myself. If I was sentenced to jail, I did not want my mother to witness that. After my lawyer made a passionate plea, the judge gave her a soliloquy and sentenced me to one year of house arrest. Her final words to me were, "I read your letter. You speak well, you have a gift. Use it to take care of your children." It would be nearly 15 years before I started to use my writing gift in a way that could take care of my children.

I have tried to hide this part of my testimony from the history books. First, to protect my relationship with my children, fearing they wouldn't look at me the same, and then feeling embarrassed for them. But the more I am rooted and grounded in Christ, the more I am free to share all of my mess! There is someone who has a similar story and is probably right in the middle of it thinking, "How did I get here?" Well, when I sat in that central cellblock hours after my house arrest sentencing, I asked myself that very same question. The worst part of my father, the very thing my mother left him for, is the very thing I had in me. He was a bank robber; a professional one at that. The final straw for my mother was when he used her car as a getaway vehicle. My mother ended up in a police lineup. She wanted a better life for me; yet, for a moment, I was just like my father.

But, God has a way of creating a new thing in you. When you make a commitment to be Souled Out for God and not man or material things, all things work together for good. I stand on the promises of a Savior who saved me from myself. He does not see my sin. Instead, He sees His Son who died for me. When I began to separate my identity, who I am and who God is creating me to be, I received peace. Being Souled Out for God means that I no longer work for the enemy. It means trusting in Him completely. It means no longer looking at my problems as mountains, but placing my focus on the only one who can solve them. I am no longer ashamed of who I used to be. I am fearfully and wonderfully made, and each day I live knowing that nothing I do can take away the love of Jesus.

From Invisible to Visible

CYNTHIA FOX EVERETT

*"Then Peter said, 'Silver and gold I do not have, but what I do have
I give you: In the name of Jesus of Nazareth, rise up and walk.'"*

Acts 3:6 (NKJV)

Before the loss of my brother, I thought that I had my past in a box tucked away in the back of my mind; at least that's what I told myself. This one incident would alter my life and mind forever. It would set in motion a chain of events that would somehow take control of my life. When I ran from God, I didn't expect to run back into Him. He was waiting patiently.

After the murder of my youngest brother on December 18, 1999, my life and my mind took on a new form and twist. No one was ever arrested and charged for his death and I was beyond angry. I spent the next three years outraged and bitter. I was almost self-destructive. No one wanted to be angry with me, so I helped myself. My husband said to get over it because what I was doing wasn't healthy.

It seemed like everyone went on with their lives except for me. I allowed my youngest brother's death to affect my marriage and my relationships with my siblings and parents. It also showed me the places in my life I thought I had under control. Things just started to come out of the woodwork. I knew in my spirit that God was the only person who could help me. I was very angry at Him for taking my brother. I knew the anger didn't make sense and I was blaming the wrong person; but, I had to be mad at someone. I was already beating myself up and I needed more company. I am grateful that God isn't like man. My brother's death seemed to trigger things that I dealt with in the Desert Shield/Desert Storm War in 1990-1991. The place I'd put those emotions when I didn't want to deal with them was no longer hidden. I knew that I needed help, but didn't quite know how to go about getting it; so, I kept my feelings a secret. I was very ashamed that I didn't have it all together like everybody else did. The more I looked for answers on how to handle things myself, the more confused I became. It was bigger than me. I wondered if God was mad at me because I was angry at Him. I didn't want to get professional help because I was so embarrassed and ashamed. Who was I going to talk to about depression and suicide without being judged? I soon found out.

I was raised in church. My father is a minister. I galloped from church after the birth of my first child at 17. I ran until 2003 when I visited a coworker's church. The pastor stated, "Follow me as I follow Christ." I said to myself, "I can do that." Even though I had given up on God, He didn't give up on me. I had done such a miserable job of managing my life that I had nothing to lose and everything to gain. I chased and tried everything but God. After my first year in the ministry,

I made up my mind that nothing was going to separate me from the Word of God again. I've been there for 14 years and counting. Since I was raised in the church I thought I knew quite a bit, but I had a lot to learn. I remember feeling the Holy Spirit for the first time; it was amazing. I searched for more of it. I thought, "As long as I feel this feeling I will be ok." Little did I know, it wasn't quite that easy. The more I thought I knew, the less I knew.

In 2003, I was diagnosed with depression due to PTSD (Post-Traumatic Stress Disorder) and started taking various psychotropic drugs. My journey with mental illness was official and recorded. Little did I know how hard it would be to conquer mental illness without almost forfeiting my sanity, mind, body, and soul. The doctors were trying different combinations of medication mixed with individual and group therapy. On October 4, 2006, I was involved in a car accident that sent me spinning into a whirlwind romance with pain medicines. Over the next few years, I developed an addiction to them. By 2008, I was taking four different narcotics for pain and anxiety, and I was also taking sleep meds. I was getting my meds from five different doctors. They didn't know about each other. With all of this going on, I was still serving God faithfully in the church and never missing a service.

A close friend knew about my addiction, but she kept my secret. I hid it well because I was ashamed. I didn't have a lot of people to trust and I really couldn't talk to anyone at church. I felt that if they knew, they would kick me out of the church and never speak to me again. My close friend and I fasted and prayed for my deliverance, but I wasn't strong enough to do it on my own. I always thought about the stigmas that come with mental illness, not to mention being a black woman. My mother would always tell me how strong the women in my family are. I would never tell her that I wasn't that strong, so I dealt with it the best way I knew how.

Little did I know that God had His own plans for me. He still covered me with His grace and mercy. I started to believe that He would never leave me or forsake me. My faith in Him was strengthened every day. The enemy would try to get me to doubt God, His Word, and myself; but, that pushed me closer to God rather than away from Him. I was separated from my husband, and my children lived with him. I had lost another brother, this time to heart disease. As the oldest of six children, my responsibilities in this capacity were starting to be more than I could bear. Since quitting wasn't an option, I dug in with the help of the Holy Spirit and started taking things by force; at least that's what I told myself and that's what others saw. When I would go home at night it was a different story. As soon as I got home I went straight to my pills. They were nonjudgmental, and they loved me. I had some in the kitchen drawer, so I wouldn't have to race to my room. Most times, they didn't kick in fast enough. Some nights I didn't quite make it to the bed. I would pull the covers off my bed and lay on the floor. Once we buried my brother, life became unbearable. I didn't have the strength or the desire to live. I couldn't do it for my children, grandchildren, parents, or siblings. I couldn't do it for anyone. Life as I knew it had been vacuumed out of me. I saw it as a good thing. I secretly prayed that God would have mercy on me, and go ahead and let me die in my anguish. It didn't quite work out like that.

One Sunday after church, I felt like I had all the planets on my shoulders. I was done. I went home and mixed up a pill cocktail. I took all my meds at once—about 15 pills. At this point, I had stopped eating and was taking my meds on an empty stomach. It didn't take long for them to take effect. I remember dozing off to sleep and I didn't wake up until the next day. I was scared and disappointed. The enemy taunted me and said that I couldn't even kill myself and I heard laughter in my ear. With my back to the wall, determined to die, I doubled up on my pills. I was going to have the last word. I filled the tub with hot water and put some anointing oil in it. As soon as the pills took effect, I got into the tub. I whispered faintly, "Jesus, help me." I started sliding down into the tub and stopped when the water reached my bottom lip. God spoke to me and said that He loved me and that my life wasn't mine to take. My tears stopped suddenly. He told me that He allowed me to go through all that I went through. He then told me to write and tell others that the only way to make it through life was through Him. I had started writing after the death of my first brother. That's the only way I could deal with it. Everybody told me to get over it; but, I didn't know how to do that, and no one seemed to be able to tell me.

On August 25, 2008, I checked myself into detox for seven days and rehab for a month. I chose that day because it was the birthday of my second deceased brother. Alcohol and drugs contributed to his death. I had to come clean with myself and the doctors. I had to confess my dirty little secret out loud. I didn't recognize myself or my behavior; even the pain was unrecognizable. My skin, bones, joints, and muscles were pulling in different directions. It felt like my legs were walking without me. I asked God for forgiveness and to stop the mental, physical, and emotional pains that had merged and taken over my life. He reminded me that Jesus paid the price for everything we had to go through and that I just had to walk it out. I rocked myself to sleep and prayed.

In June 2014, I abruptly stopped taking the medications I was receiving from three different doctors. They were interacting negatively, but no one would change them; so, I stopped taking them on my own. I ended up in the ER and then in the hospital for three long days. They stabilized me and sent me home, with no meds, to wrestle with the demons of my past, my failures, and my dreams that I could no longer control. I started to interact with my dreams. Iraqi soldiers were shooting at me while I hid behind my pillows. A dirty, bloody, injured Saudi Arabian mother and her daughter were at the foot of my bed. They were bigger than life to me. She kept asking me why I killed her daughter. With tears in my eyes, I tried to convince her that I didn't mean to, that I didn't have a choice. I insisted that I was sorry. She kept repeating the same thing to me. I buried my face into my already soaked pillow and started to pray to my faithful Father while hoping that He didn't remember when I was so angry at Him. I kept asking God to please help me to wake up and make them disappear. I almost lost my breath because I was holding the pillow tightly over my face. It felt like I had fainted, but I hadn't. I was afraid to go to sleep. I was exhausted, in every way imaginable, from not sleeping or eating. I was so exhausted that I was forgetting to take my medicine. I lived alone, and I fell down the stairs a few times.

In July/August 2014, I knew I couldn't live this way anymore. With strength from God, I was able to be proactive instead of reactive. At this point, I had a personal relationship with Christ and I knew that He would never leave me or forsake me. This I knew for sure and no one, no pills, nor my past could take that away from me. I made a call to my pastor and we discussed my options and prayed. That was the support I needed, along with my parents and children. I made a call to The Emotional Crisis Hotline at the Veteran's Medical Center. They were expecting me. This time, I was prepared to fight even harder for my life and my anointing. I spent 12 days there. I wasn't leaving until I got things right. The Holy Spirit, my pastor, and my family were with me every step of the way. I had to change my medication again. I got rid of the narcotics and got something milder. I learned to cope with the issues going on in my world. I changed my perspective on a lot of things that were going on in my life. I started forgiving others, but mainly I forgave myself. I learned that until you forgive yourself, your journey will be exceptionally hard to finish. I figured that if God could forgive me for my past then I could forgive me too.

It has taken time, but I did it through sound counseling from my pastor along with prayer and fasting. It should have taken three to four months to finish this round of therapy, but it took me almost three years. I believe I was right where I needed to be. No matter where I have been in my life, I know that God has never left my side even when I tried to leave Him. I threw in the towel and He threw it back. Once I took away the shame in my mind, I was ready to heal. My life and journey was what it was. Only by God's grace and mercy have I made it this far, and I will keep pressing toward Him. I realized I was much stronger than I thought. I stopped looking at me and started focusing on helping someone else. God doesn't waste anything we go through in life, not even our tears. I learned to find "Cynthia" in others. I'm learning to look at others like God sees them. I realize that it is truly a privilege and honor for God to trust you with an anointing, and I don't take it for granted. I'm glad that God didn't give up on me while I was going through life, even though I gave up on myself. I know without a doubt that He is faithful and true to His word. I don't know where I would be without His unfailing love.

A soulful reflection: "Wounds don't heal the way you want them to, they heal the way they need to. It takes time for wounds to fade into scars. It takes time for the process of healing to take place. Give yourself that time. Give yourself that grace. Be gentle with your wounds. Be gentle with your heart. You deserve to heal."—Dele Olanubi

A Happy Soul

NICOLE MATTHEWS

*"You lead me in the path of life; I experience absolute joy
in your presence; you always give me sheer delight."*

Psalm 16:11 (NET)

A happy soul can guide you through the darkest circum-
stance without the residual effects of negativity but with
profound understanding. I struggled with depression for
many years. I questioned myself, an occasional therapist,
and often asked God, "Why do I feel this way?" while praying
to be released from my prison of sadness and despair.

I was so fed up and exhausted with sadness that one
night I stood up in Bible Study and announced to the congregation that I was struggling with depression. I hoped to
be cured or at least have the correct prayer prayed over me.
The response I received was shocking, to say the least. I was
confronted with gasps, and looks of judgment and distaste.
One person even said, "I'm glad you didn't kill yourself." It
truly amazed me that even "these people" who professed to
know God had such misconceptions about depression. It
surprised me because the Bible spoke continuously about
people being depressed and low in spirit at different times in

their lives; so, why didn't they (these professed Bible readers and Scripture quoters) understand me or the valley I was trotting in? I believe they didn't understand because they bought into the overwhelming misconception and stigma of mental health perpetuated by today's society and our churches collectively. These stigmas are fueled by fear and lack of knowledge. My experience left me feeling lost and alone. I began to feel ashamed and sunk down into my seat, praying for magical powers so I could just vanish.

Can you imagine going into the hospital because you are having a heart attack only to be told you can't get help until you die? Well, that is how I felt. It was at that point that I realized two things: 1) I was doomed forever. Then, oddly I realized: 2) It was up to me to figure out another way to help myself. I had become vulnerable and placed my expectations where they did not belong. I expected healing from those who were not able to heal. That is not to say we are not accountable for each other, but there are times when you are left alone on purpose for a purpose.

That incident kept me out of church for nine months. During my time away from the church, something great happened—I got closer to God than I had ever been before. I was encouraged to read my Bible, which led me to understand and to connect with God on another level. I read chapters and wrote my interpretations of them. I wrote devotions. It was amazing. During this time, I gained spiritual clarity and understanding during my journey through darkness and despair. It was liberating. That resting period on my journey to greatness created my foundation of a happy soul. I learned how to regain and maintain my joy.

In that period of darkness and despair, I felt most alone. It was as if He had forsaken me to live in a dark wilderness forever. Coincidently, it was during that same period that I realized I was not alone. I was reminded, through vivid memories, of times when others felt God had turned His back on them and I was able to see God in their lives and point out His presence. How odd that I could see God on every life but my own, or was it odd?

I'm going to share a profound day in my life. It was the day I beat up a police officer. Yes, you read it right. There was a time in my life when I had a quick temper and I didn't care who you were. Thank God for change, but back to this amazing event. It was 12:00 p.m. and I was at my daughter's school. She had forgotten a homework assignment at home, so I agreed to drop it off on my way to lunch. I arrived at the school, signed in at the office, then was provided a pass and her class location for that period. As I was walking down the hallway, the Dean of Girls asked me what I was doing at the school, so I showed her the pass given to me by the office and continued on my way. By the time I made it to my daughter's class, I was greeted by four large men. Only because of their uniforms was I able to deduce that they were school security. Along with them was one police officer. I was shocked by the sight and remembered wondering what was going on at this school. I soon found out they were there for me. They started yelling at me and asking me to leave. I'm showing my pass and trying to explain why I was there. They were not interested. It was as if I had committed some awful crime. The police officer said, "This is the last time I'm going to ask you to leave." Now I'm more than confused and I'm mad. I asked, "Why do I have to leave?" That was the wrong question. Actually, they did not want me to ask any questions. The police officer put his hand on my arm then reached for his billy club.

The next thing I knew, my fist hit his face. Here we go again with my bad temper and bad choices. There was a scuffle. I was not giving up. But then my daughter appeared, so I allowed the officer to handcuff me and lead me away to the police car. During the scuffle, the officer had called for backup, so other officers met me at the police car. My thought was, "Wow! You've really done it now, Nicole." The officer who I hit advised the other officers he had everything under control. The murmurs from the officers and the school faculty were scary. They all stated that I was going to be charged with more than an assault, and someone announced I would get more time in jail because the crime happened on school property. I remember thinking, "I'm never getting out of jail." As I was being led to jail by the police officer I hit and whose nose I bloodied (who had every right not to like me, every right to lock me up and throw away the key), he did something beautiful. He began to tell me the plans God had for me. He told me God had plans for me to encourage people and how much joy I was going to bring into the lives of many. This strange man, an officer of the law whose nose would not stop bleeding because of me, used compassion to look right through me and into my soul. I believe he was looking at me through the eyes of Jesus. I cried and hollered like a baby in that car because I knew the officer was right.

We finally made it to the police station, and the officer explained that because God had plans for me, he was only charging me with trespassing. As the officer departed, he mentioned that I would be out a couple of hours after processing. There are no words to describe the joy I felt. My nonchalant attitude was, "Thank God I'm not going to jail." I went inside, took my mug shot, and patiently waited for my turn to leave. But, day turned to night and I was given pajamas, a mattress, a pillow, a blanket, and led to a jail cell. My mind was blown. What was happening? Did the officer lie to me? Was God about to let me go to jail? Fear took over my mind as we walked through the housing unit. I was no longer big, bad Nicole. I was frightened Nicole, quietly calling on God to intervene. I'm going to break right here for just a second. Things did not go as I planned, so I lost trust. I was now angry with myself, but most of all with God because He had the ability to open those jail doors and let me go home. So, as I walked into that wide, concrete space with women from all over, I felt defeated and lonely. I just wanted to disappear. I wanted my momma. As I took my space and started making up my cot, I overheard a woman say, "God is not behind these walls." I immediately turned to talk to her. I reminded her that God is everywhere even though things don't look the way you want them to look. She and I had a great conversation and other ladies joined in on our discussion. We had our own praise and worship right in the middle of that jail cell. I no longer felt alone or scared. My concern was only for this woman. I wanted to make sure she was reacquainted with hope. After a while, we decided to pray and go to sleep. Immediately after our prayer, I heard the guard say, "Matthews, roll it up. You're leaving." You know I jumped up like a lightning bolt. I said goodbye to the ladies and was on my way out. Now remember, I went into jail around 12:00 p.m. and I was finally being released at almost 5:00 a.m. I did not see the significance of that day until years later. After my release, I went to my court date for the trespassing charge. Look at how God works. When I got to court, no one even knew who I was or why I was there. It was like the incident never happened.

That day changed me. Not because I gave my life to God immediately, but it helped me to see that He is always working and to understand there is purpose in everything; I just need to trust Him. I began to work on my temper. I took inventory of my life to start making other necessary changes that would align me with the joy God had stored up just for me. I also began to focus on God and all He had done for me—the protection, the love, the forgiveness. My soul came alive. I looked at my life, took notice of what I was good at, and I realized that God gave me a heart for people and the gift to encourage them. Even while living "my life my way," I had a love for hurting people. So, I placed more focus on that. I worked on my attitude. I began to truly be grateful for the life I was given, and the grace and mercy He had shown me while I was living life according to my rules. I was able to see that it was God who kept me and not me or my big, bad attitude. So, in times of depression where nothing but darkness, unhappiness, and confusion looms around me, God steps in and allows my eyes to truly open to His work. He helped me find purpose in every incident, accident, and event that had ever happened in my life. My sadness began to lift, the clouds of confusion faded, and the darkness opened to immense light. Joy began to fill my soul with hope. Everything in my life seemed to reveal its importance in orchestrating His marvelous plan.

My happy soul does not come without work or effort. I have a daily routine that incorporates prayer, devotion, and worship. My routine keeps me focused, moving forward, and moving higher. I now set goals to change what is not good and I work on adding more good into my life. That incident brought awareness to the way I was living and directed me to change. So, at this point I am practicing being grateful, setting goals, and focusing on the goodness that is within me. Creating happy soul habits, along with prayer and reading my Bible, started me on the path back to me. Having intentional habits brought me closer to God, so much so that I gave my life back to Him. Getting baptized for the second time was the greatest moment of my life. It was even greater than birth because it was a choice I made to give my life back to the One who gave life to me.

Now, let's go back to my incident with the police officer. That situation was revealed for its exact purpose: that I must always trust God even when circumstances look bleak. I was owed the consequences of my actions; but, God stepped in and provided me with grace. God had a greater plan, not just for me but for the police officer and the woman who had completely lost hope inside of that jail cell. He used my bad decision to touch His people where we needed to be touched, while He receives all the glory. Imagine how humbling that situation had to be for the officer not to do his will but the will of our Father. Imagine how uplifted that woman felt going into a situation that by all accounts seemed dark and lonely, but God reminded her that He would be there for her. And for me, it was amazing to see God work on my behalf after I had turned my back on Him for so many years. I often ask myself, "If I were in that same situation today, what would I do differently?" And it brings me right back to God's plan for my life. I would still end up sitting here telling the story of His grace and mercy no matter what choice I made on that day in the school hallway. What would you have done? Can you imagine the amount of trouble we could relieve ourselves of if we trusted God blindly and completely? I began to change my life and limited beliefs because of many moments I recognized as God moments. Now, instead of believing my life is my own and crying over my bad breaks, relationships, and circumstances, I've adopted a new set of beliefs that leave me happier even when happy things don't happen. I have changed my environment to include more positive people—individuals who keep me focused on my God-given joy. They are there to grow me, hold me accountable, and to be witnesses of God's goodness. Trusting God and being in His presence helps me to live in the present moment; not worrying about my past or fearing my future, but appreciating the gifts and blessings He has given me today. I am also able to reflect and understand how wonderful my life is because I have breath, a closeness to God, and a happy soul.

Never Underestimate the Power of God

SILVESTER LEWIS JR.

"I was young and now I am old, yet I have never seen the righteous forsaken or their children begging bread."

Psalm 37:25 (NIV)

"Looking at them, Jesus said, 'With people it is impossible, but not with God; for all things are possible with God.'"

Mark 10:27 (NASB)

As I review and reflect on the various events that have transpired over the course of my life, I am overwhelmed with gratitude and praise to my Lord and Savior, Jesus Christ. He has been present in every peak and valley of my life and He has always had a plan and purpose for me. Job 42:2 tells us, "I know that you can do all things, and that no purpose of yours can be thwarted" (ESV). His love, grace, and mercy have often rendered me speechless and I am so grateful for all that He has done for me. When I think of His goodness, my soul cries out in complete adoration and I am compelled to share the amazing blessings that He has bestowed on me.

There are many things that I did not understand when I was a young man. However, now that I am older and more mature in Christ, I can see very clearly that God was guiding me and moving powerfully through every phase of my journey. Some phases of my journey have been more pleasant than others but whether they were bitter or sweet, God has been there through them all. It is my prayer that by reading my testimony, you witness the power of God in your own life.

When I was just a young boy, I felt as if I was different from my siblings. I felt like I was the black sheep because out of all seven of us, I was always being singled out. For example, whenever we would go outside to play, my grand-mother would instruct me to talk to her while she let my siblings go play without me. I would get mad that they were allowed to play while I was forced to listen to her lectures. I didn't want to listen to her, I wanted to go play with the other kids! She would talk to me about God for what felt like hours. She would tell me how God wanted me to live and about the Bible. I also remember my father being very hard on me. I always thought that they were picking on me, but over the years I learned that they were simply pushing me to be the best me that I could be. My father was tough on me because he wanted me to be a better man than he was. I hated it when I was younger, but now I understand what they were trying to do, and I am thankful. Is there someone in your life who challenges you to be your best?

As I got older, I got tired of my dad's constant lectures. I thought I was big and bad, and I desperately wanted to be out on my own; so, I decided to leave home when I was 16 years old. It didn't take long for me to get caught up with the wrong crowd. I learned the hard way that if you don't stand for something, you will fall for anything. So, I was 16 years old and running the streets with hustlers. Before long, I followed their lead and I started doing things I had no business doing. I was a thief, drug dealer, and hustler. I slept in parked cars or wherever I could lay my head. I knew that I had no business being around the types of people and things I was around, but I was a knucklehead and I did what I thought I wanted to do. Before long, I decided that I wanted to be a hitman. The people that I was running with were involved in everything under the sun, so I knew that it would not be hard for me to start doing that. They made it look cool and it seemed like they had lots of power and money; both things were very attractive to me.

Although I knew that nothing good could come from running the streets, I was influenced by my environment. By the grace of God, I can say that I have never taken another life and by that same grace my own life was spared. I could have easily been killed when I was in the streets doing wrong, but God was with me. When I thought I wanted to do certain things, He always had a way of protecting me. His Word tells us in Proverbs 16:25, "There is a way that seems right to a man, But its end is the way to death" (NKJV). I know that I was not headed down the right path, and I am so glad that God prevented me from doing the things I thought I wanted to do. When you look back on your life, are there things that you thought you wanted or tried to do but God prevented them from happening? Whether you realize it or not, that was God's guidance and protection. For years, I continued to run the streets. I thought I was God's gift to women, and before long I had left a trail of broken hearts. Whenever women wanted to get close to me, I pushed them away. Deep down, I didn't want to hurt anyone. I was just trying to find myself.

When I was about 18 years old, I got married. Unfortunately, my marriage didn't last long. Looking back, I can honestly say that my marriage fell apart because of me. I was too young and immature to handle the responsibility of maintaining a marriage for a long period of time. I didn't know much about life or about myself. I hate that my marriage fell apart and I was sad to do that to the children. My first wife had beautiful children and I loved them as my own. Being a father to them taught me a lot about what it means to be a man in this world. Honestly, they helped me grow up and mature into the man that I am today. I eventually had children of my own as well. What challenging experience has helped you grow and mature into the person you are today?

By the time I was 27, my years of running the streets were starting to catch up with me. I always felt tired because I never got a good night's rest. God's Word tells us in Isaiah 48:22, "'There is no peace for the wicked,' says the Lord" (NASB). I slept with one eye open because that's how it is when you're in the streets; you can't trust anyone, and you can never let your guard down. Eventually, I ran into some trouble with the law and I was facing five to ten years in jail; but, by the grace and mercy of God, I did not have to do any time.

I eventually married again, and one day one of my step-children was telling me about her experience at church. She told me that people were dancing and having a great time in the Spirit. I had never heard of anything like this, so I decided to go check the church out for myself. The following Sunday, I went to church and sat in the back. The pastor, Elder Smith, was preaching about last chances. I immediately felt a twinge in my heart because I knew that it was no coincidence that I was hearing about last chances. At the end of the service, Elder Smith had an altar call and I decided to go up and ask for prayer. When I reached the altar, Elder Smith told me to lift my hands and praise God. I was hesitant, but I followed his instructions. As I lifted my hands and closed my eyes, I felt an amazing sensation that I had never felt before. Shocked and afraid, I put my hands down. "How did that feel, Son?" Elder Smith asked. I told him that I had never felt anything like that before. It was a scary feeling because I felt as if I was no longer in control of my body. I didn't like feeling like I was not in control. Elder Smith encouraged me to lift my hands and praise God again, but to go deeper this time. I didn't know what he meant when he said to go deeper but I gave it a try. Once again, I was overwhelmed by the feeling that came over my body. At that time, I thought I was a tough guy; but, the Holy Spirit met me as I stood there at that altar. He did not care about my "wanna be tough guy" persona. He broke through that and I'm so glad that He did.

Although I didn't turn away from the wrong that I was doing immediately, my life changed forever after that day at the church. I found myself feeling led to return to the church again the next Sunday. I began reading my Bible and learning all that I could about the Scriptures I was reading. I also began to pray more often. I asked God to help me understand His teachings and principles. I also continued attending church on Sundays. The more I learned about God, the more I enjoyed what I was learning, and the more I wanted to learn even more. I was like a kid in a candy store, eager to learn all that I could about God, prayer, and His Word.

Not long after I started building my relationship with God, my church had a revival. I went every night and each night was more intriguing than the night before. I remember one preacher talking about living the way God wanted us to live. His message really touched me because I knew I had been living wrong for many years. God was teaching me that He did not want that life for me. I immediately felt great remorse for all that I had done. As I sat listening to Elder Smith, I remembered all the times my grandmother preached to me about God when I was a young boy. I started to realize that the power of God had been with me all along! You see, it is important that we understand God's power in our lives. His Word tells us in Romans 8:28-29, "And we know that all things work together for good to those who love God, to those who are the called according to His purpose. For whom He foreknew, He also predestined to be conformed to the image of His Son, that He might be the firstborn among many brethren" (NKJV). As I began to learn more about the power of God, I began to recognize His presence through-out my life. I feel overwhelmed with gratitude because He thought enough of me to be present in my life from a young age up until now even though I didn't always recognize Him.

Most recently, God showed me the greatness of His power in my health. Three years ago, I was diagnosed with Crohn's disease. I have endured many difficulties with this diagnosis, and at times my faith has been weary. There have been times when I doubted God's power because I was in so much pain. Even through this, God has remained steadfast. I praise Him because He has shown me so many things. He's taught me how to forgive others and how to grow in grace. He teaches me how to be the best version of myself and how to live the way He wants me to live. He continues to teach me things daily. I challenge you to seek God's face every day. Let Him show you the power of His Word, and most importantly the power of His love. If you look closely, you will see that His power has been with you throughout your entire life; it's just up to you to recognize it. God's Word tells us in Ephesians 3:20-21, "Now to Him who is able to do exceedingly abundantly above all that we ask or think, according to the power that works in us, to Him be glory in the church by Christ Jesus to all generations, forever and ever, Amen" (NKJV). His Word also says in Jeremiah 32:27, "I am the LORD, the God of all mankind. Is anything too hard for me?" (NIV). God's power is the greatest thing we will ever experience in this life. As long as there is breath in your body, do not underestimate it for there is nothing greater!

A Broken Soul
Revived Through Jesus

CATHERINE DAVIS WRIGHT

*"And so, dear brothers and sisters, I plead with you to give your
bodies to God because of all he has done for you. Let them
be a living and holy sacrifice—the kind he will find acceptable.
This is truly the way to worship him. Don't copy the behavior
and customs of this world, but let God transform you into a new
person by changing the way you think. Then you will learn to know
God's will for you, which is good and pleasing and perfect."*

Romans 12:1-2 (NLT)

*"Trust in the Lord with all your heart; do not depend
on your own understanding. Seek his will in all you
do, and he will show you which path to take."*

Proverbs 3:5-6 (NLT)

I am the child of a KING.

As I lay on the cold hospital bed, I can hear this Caucasian
physician tell my mother, "She's pregnant." At 12 years old,
"Is this really happening?" is all that I could say gently to

myself as I waited for my mother to return to the exam room. It was 2003 when my delicate secret was exposed: my stepbrother had been molesting me for the past year and now I was expecting a baby. Fear completely covered me as these strange doctors and nurses began examining every inch of my insides. I felt as though the entire world could see me; a young black girl from Savannah, Georgia, who was completely worthless. Merriam-Webster's Collegiate Dictionary defines worthless as useless, and that is exactly how I felt.

As the examinations continued, I was being questioned by several officers, detectives, nurses, and my mother. I was in a boxing ring, fighting against the world's number one undefeated fighter in the industry, and I was catching blow-after-blow before I could even blink. In my head I thought, "Was this not okay that my stepbrother took advantage of my juvenile innocence? Why didn't I ever open my mouth and say anything? Was I supposed to be wise at this age of my life, after all, I was preparing for the eighth grade." That hot summer would forever change our blended family, and my life would never be the same. I thought, "I surely cannot birth this child and cause he or she to live with such a dark shadow over their life. I did not want people to become silent when they saw my child coming because they were busy gossiping about how he or she was conceived." I was 12 ½ and in no shape to raise a child when I was a child myself. On the other hand, a child should be a blessing from God, right? The thoughts became too much to process. As time passed, the decision was made that an abortion would be the best choice for me and the unborn child. The household had changed for the worst, and the arguments between my mother and stepfather were countless. My younger sister and I knew that this was not what family was about. I began feeling like I did not matter to anyone, despite how much my mother said I did. Life was pointless. I killed my child, and there was no reason to live anymore. I ruined the family that was still new, and I felt that everything was all my fault. After months of counseling and group therapy, I began to feel like things were going to be okay, but I was clearly mistaken.

In 2006, my stepbrother was released from prison and re-entered the home. My mind began racing and my feet began to pace across the green and white tiled kitchen floor. I wondered, "Why must I see him now and how am I supposed to feel at this moment?" My therapist had explained to me over and over again that child sexual abuse was not okay, so why did I feel numb? "Pack up some clothes, now," my mother said, annoyed. My younger sister looked at me confused as we began to pack. My mother, younger sister, and I were leaving our house to drive to my grandmother's house in South Carolina. For about a month, my mother's white 2000 Ford Expedition was our closet. "Are you kidding me? We're really living with my grandmother and storing things in our car, while he gets to sleep peacefully?" I said to my best friend in high school. That point of my life was when I became rebellious.

During my freshman year of college, I met my daughter's father; he was considered a drug dealer. I was intrigued by this bad guy who had lust in his eyes for me. My adrenaline was at an all-time high and all I could think about was being his "ride or die." Smoking weed, skipping class, drinking, and clubbing non-stop became a trend for me. I felt as though I was alive again for the first time in many years. I did not care that it was not safe to drink and drive, nor did I care about any of my unappealing behaviors. All I knew was that I'd been through entirely too much in my youth and now I was grown and could make my own decisions. On the other hand, deep down inside, there was hurt, anguish, devastation, and depression hidden beneath all the layers that I created. Here I was thrilled with life, and now pregnant again at the age of 19. "Wow, there must actually be a God," was my initial response to my cousin because since the abortion, I felt that I would never be able to have children after putting my body through so much at an early age.

There were many complications throughout my pregnancy, and I believed that it was a punishment from God for all the negative things I had done recently. I was physically abused by my daughter's father, arrested for driving in his illegal cars, and lonely. I knew that life had to be better than the hand that I was being dealt. My mother began talking to me about how life was going to change drastically once my daughter was born, so I had to decide what type of mother I wanted to be. I was confused because for so many years I felt like an emotionless, unworthy being, and now I had to be a mother, which was something I was unsure that I could do. I thought, "Am I able to give this child the love that she needs?" The devil was speaking to me in so many ways it appeared that I was losing my sanity at times. I was angry for so many reasons. Why did my mother stay with my step-dad after that tragic incident? Why was my father never truly present in my life? Would my life have been different if my dad was there full-time to teach me life skills? What if

I would have spoken up when things first began to happen with my stepbrother? I was furious and wanted answers!

On April 17, 2010, my daughter Cayden was born and at that very moment I knew that it was not about me anymore. I was blessed with a beautiful child despite what the devil wanted me to believe. I had to pray to God and ask for forgiveness immediately. I knew that my soul was lost, and God would be the only one who could save me. I needed to be healed from the hurt of losing a child. I did not realize how much that haunted me to that very day. I demanded that God teach me how to forgive. I needed those heavy burdens lifted off me before I held my daughter in my arms. I did not want her to feel heaviness instead of love and comfort. When I held Cayden for the first time, I knew that God had done the lifting and I was able to experience a true love that I never could have imagined.

Self-Reflection:

For many years, being sexually abused and conceiving a child at the age of 12 was not an easy thing for me to deal with emotionally and mentally. That major incident created a negative ripple effect: drugs, alcohol, and sex. My mother once told me, "If a man runs down the street naked, people will say, 'Look at that fool.' But, if a woman runs down the street naked, people will say, 'Look at that whore.'" I knew this was wisdom that she was instilling in me, but how could anything stick with a 12-year-old girl who felt she had no soul? Now that I am approaching 27 years old, I've realized that was a true quote. People tend to judge you while not even knowing your history; that can be a difficult pill to swallow. However, Jesus is who can get you through any situation!

I once hated life and felt as though there was no purpose for my existence. Oh my, was I wrong! Jeremiah 29:11 says, "For I know the plans I have for you," says the Lord. "They are plans for good and not for disaster, to give you a future and a hope" (NLT). God has a purpose for each of our lives. We are destined for greatness. Jeremiah 1:5 states, "I knew you before I formed you in your mother's womb. Before you were born I set you apart and appointed you as my prophet to the nations" (NLT). Granted, we may have to go through some uncomfortable journeys in our lives, but we can still be who He has called us to be if we yield to Him alone. God will never put more on us than we can handle, and I had to realize that. I lost trust in God between the ages of 11-18 and that was one of my biggest mistakes. It was not that I never spoke up, it was that I welcomed the enemy into my life with open arms.

God has always been my protector and healer. He has never left me. He knows my thoughts and He sees my heart. I had to experience the things I went through at an early age to be the woman I am today. Without those experiences, I am not sure exactly where I would be. Those valleys were how I began to learn that I must trust God with everything and not just some things. I am the child of a king. So, no matter what you go through or how bad things seem at times, believe that God is who He says He is. John 10:10 says, "The thief's purpose is to steal and kill and destroy. My purpose is to give them a rich and satisfying life." (NLT). God delivered me from my wicked ways and blessed me abundantly, especially once I forgave everyone who I felt harmed me. I completed college as a single mother and graduated with my Master's in Business Administration while working full-time. I am a leader at a major healthcare organization and actively working with youth in the church, teaching them about the right path. Although those valleys were difficult, my mother was always there for my sister, my daughter, and I. She is a true woman of God and I admire her everyday as I see her Christian walk. My younger sister is striving in Atlanta and recently graduated with her Bachelor's Degree. God has sent me an amazing, God-fearing husband, Will, who adores not only me but my daughter as well. God continues to show my family favor and I am truly thankful. He is the same God yesterday, today, and tomorrow.

Souled Out Reflection:
Still I Rise by Maya Angelou

You may shoot me with your words,
You may cut me with your eyes,
You may kill me with your hatefulness,
But still, like air, I'll rise.

His Soldier

"Repay no one evil for evil, but give thought to do what is honorable in the sight of all. If possible, so far as it depends on you, live peaceably with all. Beloved, never avenge yourselves, but leave it to the wrath of God, for it is written, 'Vengeance is mine, I will repay, says the Lord.' To the contrary, 'if your enemy is hungry, feed him; if he is thirsty, give him something to drink; for by so doing you will heap burning coals on his head.' Do not be overcome by evil, but overcome evil with good."

Romans 12:17-21 (ESV)

When I think of my Souled Out journey, I think of three phases of my life in the name of the Father, the Son, and the Holy Spirit. Phase one would be me as "that child." Phase two would be me as "that earthly soldier." And phase three would be me as "that kingdom-bound soldier."

Phase One: Souled Out as a Child

Literally, I was raised as "that child." Yes, the one who was a coincidence, the one born out of matrimony, the one who was unknowingly being raised by her grandparents until the birth mother knocked on the door and stated, "I am here to claim my daughter." Therefore, my first transformation took place at the age of five. Confusingly, my biological mother removed me from the dwelling of my grandparents (my father's parents). I was not familiar with the dynamics of family relationship at that age. I only knew that my grandmother and I were inseparable. She loved me as if I were her precious princess. Her presence in my life was genuine and loving; the kind of kinship that should come from one's birth mother. The transformation made me feel extremely hurt, angry, bitter, lonely, and more than anything afraid and frightened. I was the one who later cried out to be loved unconditionally (just as her grandparent had loved her), yet no one was listening. Better yet, I was that child who attempted to run away at the age of 12, but offered her life to Christ instead.

Upon giving my life to Christ, I would like to believe that I was Souled Out! Coming to Him at such a pivotal time in my childhood granted me revelation to a genuine, spiritual being that felt more natural than anything I had ever encountered. I desired more of His presence, and I had a thirst to read and retain the information I retrieved from the B.I.B.L.E. (Basic Information Before Leaving Earth).

At this phase of my life, I am Souled Out and comprehending that I belong to Him, and that I am a child of God according to His Word. As it is written in John 1:12, "But as many as received him, to them gave he power to become the sons of God, even to them that believe on his name" (KJV). I understand that I have now been baptized in the name of the Father, His Son—Jesus, and His Holy Spirit. I shared my blessing with everyone I encountered. I enjoyed my new blessings that came with this anointing. I was grateful learning that even though my upbringing was filled with blended family members who were kin to one another, being that bastard child (a name that I was called one too many times) often reminded of that Scripture, "No one born of a forbidden union may enter the assembly of the Lord" (Deuteronomy 23:2 ESV).

I am Souled Out at this phase of my life because I am eager to attend bible study and prayer meetings on Wednesday nights. I joined the youth choir and became a lead singer. I played a major role in establishing the first youth ministry at my church because I felt as though it was imperative for other children to enjoy this new birth that had changed my childhood. I joined the youth usher board. Getting involved in ministry allowed me to experience a Souled Out manifestation for His kingdom.

B.I.B.L.E.: "Heaven and earth will pass away, but my words will never pass away" (Matthew 24:35 NIV).

Prayer: Father God, allow me to love and forgive those who have sinned against me in order that I might have a Souled Out love for others like you do. In Jesus' name I pray. Amen.

Phase Two: Souled Out as a Soldier

I am Souled Out because I am surrounded by God's favor (Psalm 5:12). Certainly, I am not the only one who has experienced something traumatic in their lifetime. Although I have had many life traumas, the most horrifying trauma I experienced took place on June 26, 1996, in Saudi Arabia.

After an afternoon run with coworkers, we agreed to meet up later for a movie. When I got into my room, I went to the bathroom to prep for my shower. I sighed as usual as I drew the shower curtain because the window in the shower was a misfit. Seriously, a window in the shower freaked me out. Just as I was enjoying the feeling of the cool water bringing my body temperature down, a loud sound pierced my ears. It was a booming clatter that I will carry with me until my eyes are shut tightly forever. Before I could ask, "What was that?" a burning force came through that annoying window and tossed me from the shower onto the adjacent marbled wall.

I am Souled Out because, "Have I not commanded you? Be strong and courageous. Do not be afraid; do not be discouraged, for the LORD your God will be with you wherever you go" (Joshua 1:9 NIV).

I had no room for fear at that moment. For the most part, my leadership skills shifted into first gear immediately. Just like the Shepherd caring for His sheep, I had 45 soldiers looking up to me for answers as I looked up to the Lord. After ensuring that all 45 were safe (although some were injured) and informing them that we had just endured a terrorist attack, we began search and rescue for the less fortunate. I recalled that saying, "What would Jesus do?" and I set the example for my soldiers; leading the way (in a Souled Out way) in an attempt to locate and account for my comrades.

The aftermath of the explosion was worse than a scene from a horror movie. There was dark smoke flying, hot debris falling, horrible smells, whaling voices screaming for help, and scattered body parts (arms, legs, and heads). The building next to my window had completely vanished, while other buildings were still crumbling. I had to remain focused because I was His Souled Out soldier who others were depending on. "I spread out my hands to You; My soul longs for You like a thirsty land" (Psalm 143:6 NKJV).

I am Souled Out! "... Let the weak say, 'I am strong!'" (Joel 3:10 AMP).

Prayer: Father God, thank you for showing up in my life at times when I needed to make moral choices and own a character of righteousness. In the name of Jesus and His Holy Spirit, I am Souled Out to you. Amen.

Phase Three: Souled Out as a Kingdom-Bound Soldier

When I think of my journey, I recall one of my most life-changing Psalms. "Revive me, O Lord, for Your name's sake! For Your righteousness' sake bring my soul out of trouble. In Your mercy cut off my enemies, And destroy all those who afflict my soul; For I am Your servant" (Psalm 143:11-12 NKJV).

I retired from the United States Army with honors. So, I realize I have conquered more in life than I had ever hoped to; however, I have failed at several endeavors as well. My most unforgettable disappointment was my first marriage. You see, I vowed to have that storybook marriage. I wanted a family to call my very own. I married my first husband twice, yes, twice. We met in the Army on our first overseas assignment: Korea. He proposed to me prior to our departure. We got married in order to get our first stateside assignment (Fort Lewis, Washington) together as husband and wife. We kept our marriage a secret, especially from his family because his mother wanted us to have a formal wedding. Not only did we have that second wedding, but I was four months pregnant on that lovely day. I remember going on a routine appointment and having horrible cramps. I managed to get to the hospital; however, I began hemorrhaging (which is worse than bleeding). I was oblivious yet troubled by what I was experiencing. Upon seeing my doctor, she informed me that I had suffered a miscarriage. This was very excruciating! I cried for months. I still have those, "What if?" thoughts. There's not a Mother's Day that goes by that I don't reminisce. I can only imagine how Mary felt when she observed the death of her son, Jesus, hanging on a cross.

My pain didn't end with the loss of our baby. Finding out that my husband was involved with other women was heartbreaking. And worse, finding them asleep in the same bed nearly took me over the edge. I was beyond devastated. Plus, I was not educated on how to handle adultery nor did I have anyone to turn to. I stopped speaking to my husband for nearly six months. I knew he loved me, but he couldn't stop his desires of being with other women. To have other women tell me that they or their girlfriend had a sexual encounter with my husband was completely inexcusable. I felt as though he wanted permission to have concubines. I was too embarrassed to ask for a divorce because I wholeheartedly wanted the picture perfect marriage. As I was updating my professional records one afternoon, I recall one of my best friends (who had been married several times) telling me that trash belongs outside. Then, another friend said, "Lips that touch slime will never touch mine." However, I loved this man and his family with everything in me. Although my heart ached fiercely, I was torn between love and infidelity. I felt that little girl (who had once endured a transformation from hurt, bitterness, loneliness, and being afraid and frightened) seeking freedom and intentional transformation once again; so, I forgave him and divorced him. Then, I became Souled Out to Christ until He blessed me with a husband who wanted a wife who was also Souled Out to Him.

My overall life lesson is that the difference between who you are and who you want to be is what you do. I choose to be in His presence (at His feet) throughout my trials and tribulations because of who is in me and what He did for me. I choose to be Souled Out for Him. Jim Rohn stated, "Your life does not get better by chance, it gets better by change!" I honestly can't find it in my heart to be angry with anyone. You see, Jesus' last words were something like, "Forgive them Father for they know not what they do" (Luke 23:34). So, as I dwell on my three life phases: a child, a soldier, and a kingdom soldier, I ask forgiveness for those who did not know, including myself. I am Souled Out!

Vulnerable in a Storm

DENISE POLOTE-KELLY

"You rejoice in this, though now for a short time you have had to struggle in various trials so that the genuineness of your faith - more valuable than gold, which perishes though refined by fire - may result in praise, glory, and honor at the revelation of Jesus Christ."

1 Peter 1:6-7 (HCSB)

vul·ner·a·ble

Adjective:
1. Susceptible to physical or emotional attack or harm. "We were in a vulnerable position."
1.1 (of a person) in need of special care, support, or protection because of age, disability, or risk of abuse or neglect.

Synonyms:
helpless, defenseless, powerless, impotent, weak, susceptible
"He was scared and vulnerable."

My mind goes back eight years ago to a day when I was driving in a terrible rainstorm. The rain was blinding, and I wanted to pull off the road and wait until the storm passed. I recall the rain coming down so hard it was difficult to see the vehicles in front of me. It's human nature to want to stop when things become difficult to handle or understand. The definition of vulnerable illustrates exactly where I found myself. I was in a mental place of vulnerability and I was not ready to face the storm.

I recall my dear friend, Margaret, saying, "Don't stop. We don't know what may happen if we pull over." I heard the voice of God say, "Keep going. I've got you." I wanted to stop because I could not see on the side of me, in front of me, nor behind me. All I could see was rain pouring down all around us. As we continued to travel, big trucks passed us with their flashers on; but, when they got five feet ahead of me, the rear lights disappeared as if the truck was not there. The rain was getting worse instead of better. I wasn't saying much, but on the inside, I wanted to give up. I wanted to stop.

Again, Margaret said, "Don't stop" and God said, "I've got you." I was talking to myself under my breath saying, "At the next break in the rain, I'm pulling over. This rain is getting harder and I can't see." I was afraid. I was not only responsible for myself in this storm, but also Margaret and my granddaughter, MaCail. I remember thinking, "If I can't see the people around me, chances are they can't see me. One of these cars may hit us from the side or the rear because this is really a bad storm." Our natural impulse while driving in a storm is to pull over and wait.

During that time, I was challenged to keep moving forward or stop. I chose to keep going. God said, "I've got you" and my friend confirmed that simple but powerful statement. We as children of God must learn to trust that He is ever present, and He knows all about what we are faced with and challenged in. I've learned that in a time of preparation, we need to recognize the test and decide to fail or succeed. For me, failure is not an option; therefore, I keep moving through the storms.

By choosing to move through that storm, I was reminded that if I kept moving ahead I would get out of the storm but if I pulled over I might be stuck on the side of the road for a while. I was reminded that the sun would shine eventually because the rain doesn't last forever. Life is strange, and by making simple choices and decisions on our daily journey, we (believe it or not) tell God, "I trust you" or "I don't trust you." Our actions and reactions sometimes show God how vulnerable we have become. God being God will show Himself to be all that we need in those moments. He will lead us out of the wet, dark places into the beautiful, dry, lit place. He will cover us like a big umbrella.

I can think back on some storms I chose to keep moving through and other storms I was too weak to realize God was there pushing me through. My forward movement and refusal to stay stuck gave God just what He wanted from me, and that was to use me as a willing vessel. When I thought I needed to pull over, He had already poured the power of a warrior into me; therefore, I could not stop. Even when I was fearful, He made me fearless so I could keep moving.

Right now, I have four dear friends/sisters who are in a battle and I pray they hear me in their ears saying, "Keep moving, don't stop. I'm with you, and most importantly God's got you." There is no winning if you quit; therefore, we must keep moving. When I was faced with the biggest storm of my life, I didn't realize that God had already prepared me when He brought me through the raindrops. When I think back, I don't minimalize any of the obstacles I have overcome; I have simply learned the difference. He has prepared me for what is to be. I know that the plan for our lives is to follow God while not forgetting that He made the plan and He does not need our input.

When we are faced with life's challenges, and there will be a few, the thought of a pilot waiting to take off comes to mind. We are on the runway of life waiting but moving. We are in a holding pattern and soon we will be cleared for takeoff. Some of us will have to wait for a while because we have some engine problems. What that means is: when we have not made time for God (we haven't studied the Word and firmed up our foundation, we haven't taken the time to seek Him for counsel, we haven't fasted and prayed), we make it necessary to be in an extended holding pattern. These steps are important and necessary for kingdom-minded people; and as believers, the kingdom should forever be on our minds and in your hearts.

God desires our praise and He wants to reward us. The Word tells us in Galatians 6:9, "And let us not be weary in well doing: for in due season we shall reap, if we faint not" (KJV).

Being vulnerable in the storm will cause you to lose your place in line, and at this stage of our lives we can't afford to lose our place. It is time for us to stand up boldly and walk in the purpose for which God made us. We must hold up the bloodstained banner and move forward.

Jesus died that we might have life and have it more abundantly. We must not let His dying for us be in vain. The sacrifice of the perfect one should make us think about serving God without ceasing. We cannot remain helpless—needing care to recognize what an awesome privilege it is to have God love us.

To be vulnerable may also mean that you are being honest, afraid, broken, and weak about the challenges of life and everything that is discouraging you. Vulnerability encompasses guilt from the past, low self-esteem, loneliness, sadness, and a lack of joy, peace, hope and love. We may even doubt God and His ability to be more than enough in our lives when we are feeling overwhelmed. We may find ourselves doubting if He is with us in the storm. The disciples were closest to Jesus and even they doubted. I often think of the story in the Bible where Jesus was in the boat and there was a storm out on the ocean. His words were simply, "Peace, be still...and there was a great calm" (Mark 4:39 KJV).

I continued to drive that day. I did not stop. As God had planned, a few miles up the road the rain slowed down. I could see in front and all around me. He made the sun so bright I needed to put on my shades. God does just that with the challenges and disappointments in our lives. The storm does not last forever, and when we come through we should recognize that God is right there with us.

He promised to never leave us nor forsake us, and when we can't see our hands in front of our face that is truly when we need to trust God with our whole heart. He will cover us like a big umbrella and we won't even get wet. God is so wonderful in and out of the storm. He wants us to stay in the boat and allow Him to calm the storm.

Don't stop in the storm; just slow down and keep moving forward. At our weakest, God is strong. And when the rain stops, He was there all the time.

The storms in our lives can be calmed by the wave of His hand when we make up our mind to trust God to be God. He didn't ask us to walk on water. He didn't ask us to calm the storm. He merely desires our trust and praise.

The Portrait of Life: The Me I See, The Me They See, and The Me God Sees

DONNA DAVIS-CURRY

"I will praise thee; for I am fearfully and wonderfully made: marvelous are thy works; and that my soul knoweth right well."

Psalm 139:14 (KJV)

It's enlightening to know that I am being watched from three vantage points: the me I see, the me they see, and the me God sees. Some of us have been living undercover, serving as secret agents, taking on the persona of 007. But who are we really? We have been given a blank canvas, the paint, and the brushes. What will our portrait of life look like when that great day comes, and God calls us home from our labor to reward? As I have stated, there are at least three vantage points of our lives that we must look at: the me I see, the me they see, and the me God sees.

*The Me I See

Some of us see ourselves as a humble lamb, a great wife, mother, daughter, sister, and friend.

We may see ourselves as a great church worker and advocate for the kingdom of God. This is what some of us may see on the very surface of our lives; however, when the mirror has been raised in front of our faces and we look beyond the image we see, we find a deeper reflection looking back at us. We may see the reflection of broken places, deep despair, a heavy load of problems, and an anxiety mountain that seems to never move. Even though we may have a touch of faith, we do not understand why we are still blocked from the sunlight.

How is Your Portrait Looking Now?
*The Me They See

This viewpoint can be two-fold:

1. Someone may see you as a well-put-together matriarch of your family, the pillar of the community, or the fairy god-mother/god-father.

You may present yourself as one that is well dressed with not a hair out of place, the best vehicles, best neighborhood, best education, and the smartest children. Each time someone sees you, they put you as one of the top individuals they know.

2. Someone may have a vendetta against you because of your successes.

You work hard to show the world that you are indeed put together and have everything that you could ever ask for, only to find out that the very people who smile with you and say they wish great success for you are indeed hoping that your world will crumble and fall. They may see you as a know it all, a busybody, and someone who is over-compensating with your accolades because they might also see your emptiness, hurt, and pain. The unfortunate fact of this viewpoint is that you may discover the real truths behind some of your relationships through their gossip about you.

How is Your Portrait of Life Looking So Far?
*The Me God Sees

We want to show God that we are holy, that we are committed to going to church Sunday after Sunday. We work on every auxiliary/ministry that we can at the church. We make sure that we oversee every program; but the fact is, God really sees a lonely individual just trying to save face. He knows that our home and work life aren't what we pretend.

During my years in ministry, I've encountered all types of stories, from all angles, from individuals that I have counseled or met randomly. Our common denominator (myself included) is getting caught in the whirlwinds of life and not always being sure how to get out, especially unscathed. I've even dealt with individuals consumed with thinking that it's okay to tear each other down. They even tried destroying the reputation of others because of jealousy.

My message is always that we should have unity and togetherness, not division. Therefore, we should humble ourselves first; we must show humility. It's easy to show humility when we have love in our heart. "Love worketh no ill to his neighbour: therefore love is the fulfilling of the law" (Romans 13:10 KJV). The depth of humility is the height of love. That means the more love you have, the humbler you become.

Beloved friend, we have gotten so accustomed to labels and what people say about our lives that we miss what God says and what God sees within us. It doesn't matter if someone is talking about you when you are showing kindness to someone else; that's the height of love. God loved us so much that He sent His Son. Yes, it is that love that created us, that love that formed us. We are fearfully and wonderfully made. We are a design original. God was so intricate in designing each one of us.

Archos is the Greek word for master. God is our Master Architect. We should marvel at the thought that our Creator's work is admirable. "Marvelous are thy works; and that my soul knoweth right well" (Psalm 139:14 KJV). The knowledge that God created us with a divine design leads us to also believe that He created us with a divine purpose.

I found out in my spiritual walk with God that I owe Him the best portrait of me. Do you remember when we would take school pictures, and the day we got them back all our family and friends wanted one? Oh, how we couldn't wait to disburse our pictures to everyone, especially the wallet size, because we wanted to make sure that we were always carried around by everyone that loves us. It meant even more to us if we knew the picture was exceptionally cute.

We should also have that warm feeling within our hearts with our portrait of life. We should want the canvas of our daily living to represent the original divine design that God has created us to be. We should want to show off the grace and mercy God has allowed us to have once more in our lives.

Unfortunately, we have been painting our portrait without adding God to the canvas; yet, we always want to add people, places, and things. The sad thing is, we've allowed some people to grace our canvas who should never have remained in our lives after a season. God allows people to have a season in our lives. Our issue is that we never want to let people leave, even if they should go.

I've come to learn that as a believer of God, I cannot be removed from His supporting, comforting, and sovereign presence. I've matured as a Christian, and during this maturity my intimacy with God has grown. There is such a pure, agape love that gives me 20/20 vision and a clear frequency of what God has been showing and speaking to me.

I know without a shadow of a doubt that God has been the keeper of my soul. Yes, this vantage point serves as a better view for my life. I know that it will serve as a better view for you as well.

We can be filled with the Spirit of God, but not controlled by the Spirit of God. You must mature to the place where you think you are and allow the Spirit to become who He is in your life.

We need to allow God to stretch us so that we can go into another dimension in Him. I want the me God sees to be a more fulfilled, strong, yet humble woman. I want to be in a place to understand that the tools that God has given me to paint my life are being used correctly.

First thing's first, I must be completely Souled Out to Him. I must remain true to who God has created me to be. "Before I formed thee in the belly I knew thee; and before thou camest forth out of the womb I sanctified thee, and I ordained thee a prophet unto the nations" (Jeremiah 1:5 KJV). Jeremiah 1:5 reminds me that God created me with me in mind. I was going to be the only me with my set of hand prints, and now I must generate my soul print. I must live out the promises God has for me.

"For I know the thoughts that I think toward you, saith the LORD, thoughts of peace, and not of evil, to give you an expected end" Jeremiah 29:11 (KJV). God knows what our purposes are; we must now get in alignment with the plans He has for our lives. Knowing that God has formed us with a purpose is the most humbling thought. "Form" in Greek isn't speaking of shape; it is referring to a philosophical concept, the expression of being, which carries a distinctive nature or character of an individual or the being of whom it pertains.

Thus, permanently identified in that nature and character, each one of us carry a form or an essence within us. You cannot probe into my essence, but you can see the expression of my essence. You can see the expressions of our moves. In other words, people can tell who we are by how we behave; the me they see.

The expression is not independent of the essence. It is something that is within us. There is something in us that makes us express ourselves in a certain manner. Take Jesus for instance. He was in the form of God. But, understand that to be in the form of God, He's got to have the essential character of God. He can't just steal God's form for the expression to take place. He's got to have the essence. See, He would have to be in order to express.

It is impossible for God to lie. That means God cannot express who He is not. Whatever He is, that will be the form. Whatever He is inside is identical to the expression that is on the outside; yet, the form is not the essence, the form is just an expression. It is the connection to an essence that gives an expression.

Let me explain with this example: The first thing you feel from a fire is the heat. The heat is not the fire, but it is a perfect expression of the fire. As the fire increases, the heat increases. The firefighters don't put out the heat, they put out the fire. And when they put out the fire, there is no more heat. This helps me to understand painting my portrait of life better.

So, Jesus had to be God. He had to be absolute deity because He couldn't have the form of God if He was not God Himself. Therefore, in our portraits of the me I see and the me they see, we can sometimes portray ourselves as only the outward appearance. Jesus cannot go into the closet and put on God like you and I can go into our closets and put on a garment of clothing, because the garment of clothing is not essentially coming from our nature; it is something we can put on and take off. But, we cannot put on and take off who we are. We cannot put on and take off our expression; it is connected. Therefore, if we are depressed, it doesn't matter what we put on and take off, we are still depressed individuals. We could put on yellow, blue, or green. It doesn't matter because the clothes are not connected to the essential nature of who we are.

Our Savior was in the form of God—a divine essence that represents the inward being. He was the possessor of divine deity. He looked down at my mess, your mess, and the trouble we were in. Although He didn't stop being God, He possessed God. He couldn't give up His essence, but He gave up His expression. He wrapped Himself up in flesh so that He could come down to save man. That was Jesus' purpose: for you and me to come back into relationship with God the Father. He understood His purpose to give us life more abundantly.

If nothing else, I am Souled Out because of Jesus' love for you and me. I must stay the course of the purpose I was created for: to love my brothers and sisters and even my enemies, and to fulfill the gifting's God placed within me before I was formed in my mother's womb. During my trials of feeling abandoned and misunderstood, and in my times of brokenness and lonely days, I was reminded of God's grace. He carried, interceded, cared for, and loved me when I wasn't in the position to do those things for myself. I owe God everything!

God is so gracious and loving that He allows us to come back to Him and ask for forgiveness for being selfish and thinking "woe is me." We may have gotten caught up in our pain, our loss, our frustrations, or the fact that we were abused, misused, and misunderstood. We may have even dealt with an illness or are battling financial hardship. Whatever our ailments may be, He still loves us.

I love Jesus with all my heart, soul, and being. I am so grateful I understood His sacrifice for me and that I was fearfully and wonderfully made. God took the time to intricately make me a design original. My portrait of life has changed. The me I see and the me they see are now lining up with the me God sees. I am walking in my purpose to minister to the kingdom of God. My canvas has beautiful, vibrant colors that show a full life; a life of servitude, integrity, humility, and praise. Only divine connections are a part of my portrait now.

Take a self-evaluation of your portrait. What do you see? What do they see? What does God see?

*The Me I See

_____

_____

_____

_____

*The Me They See

_____

_____

_____

_____

*The Me God Sees

The Power of Purpose

KALDEJIA FAULK

There is an innate desire inside all of us to do something great in life. Deep down we all yearn to be applauded for our efforts, our accomplishments, our milestones, and our noteworthy achievements. These yearnings of praise can lead to false starts, false hopes, and false choices. False meaning doing life for the applause of others while secretly yearning for what really brings us fulfillment. True fulfillment and joy come from living a life centered and birthed through purpose.

I woke up at 44 to a stark reality. I had been, and still was, living life according to other's expectations, the media's images of what success looked like, and broken childhood dreams. I discovered I was here on the earth, close to a decade, tumbling through life half awake, half alive, and void of purpose.

As leaders, you encounter memorable moments relative to you as a leader (whether in business or ministry) daily. One such moment was being formally diagnosed with depression and anxiety. In my mind, that moment is forever etched on the canvas of life experiences that resulted in a transformation and life lesson paramount to my assignment in the earth realm. This moment would catapult me into birthing my purpose and sharing pivotal, transparent verbal and written images; a secret hidden deep in the vessel of my soul. This story-telling scenario would lend to disclosing a time of sheer darkness (though not so sheer vulnerability), feelings of guilt as well as shame, along with a host of other fleeting emotions. Here I was holding ministerial positions comprised of encouraging, inspiring, and praying for others all the while suffering in silence. How do you acknowledge an illness to those who look to you for motivation to manage and overcome life's challenges?

I discovered amid my memorable moment that I was notorious for helping others but had neglected to be an advocate for myself. While leading others to develop the skills and knowledge for meeting life's challenges, it's imperative as a leader to seek self-care first. The day I was transported by ambulance to our local hospital started just like any other workday. Mornings were full of self-talk that included having strength to make it through another day masked with a smile, encouraging words, hugs, jokes; everything other than the despair, hopelessness, loss, and anger I was feeling. Every day was comprised of a gamut of negative emotions. There was a blur between what my life appeared to be and reality. How could I continue to put the best on the outward while secretly loathing my life? To uplift and encourage others was mentally and emotionally taxing. I could see and confidently know that the best was ahead for others, but only saw failures, missed opportunities, and regrets in my forecast. My pleasantry became wishing the clock's hands moved quickly to the time of release from the daily grind of falsehood. My destination of choice became my bed. There I could sleep where the thoughts of negativity appeared to cease. A nap wasn't an hour but hours of avoiding the inevitable reality that I had been unhappy and unfilled for a long time. How long? I really had not come to terms with that. However, the space I currently occupied was beyond comfortable. In fact, it was scary. You see, this space that I never consciously occupied or knew had become a part of my repertoire. This void, empty, overwhelming, "life closing in on you" feeling was my merciless, constant, personal daily greeter, and non-favorite bedtime story.

You would think that focusing on reasons to live and things or people that bring me joy would realign me to embrace what really mattered; instead, it triggered an onslaught of negative emotions. The reason I lived, breathed, and performed in life was for the very people I didn't have the strength to emotionally or mentally be there for. The cost I was paying was beginning to take its toll. What started out emotionally and mentally taxing had now begun to manifest physically. Lack of appetite, concentration deficits, insomnia, and unexplainable aches and pains had linked arms and become a fortress. Not only were they keeping people out of my secret place, but they were now holding me hostage. Our bodies follow our thought processes and what we focus on. My focus was filled with negative thoughts and vibes which my body embraced and manifested. Our body isn't our property. It's on loan to us by the Father to manage, and to manifest our gifts, talents, and abilities to the world. My present state was robbing me of the opportunity to share my gifts, talents, and abilities with the world. I had become void of purpose. Why was I here? What had He spared my life for me to do? Who was I to impact as His representative of this journey called life? Where would I be at this juncture if this pause (this space of unease and disease with life) hadn't manifested now? When would this challenge, lack of movement, and stagnation in my life come to an end? What would this experience profit me in my journey to next (whatever that was going to look like)?

Here I was at 40 something—unfilled in life although it was moving at a rapid pace. Months seemed to have magically culminated and morphed into a picture I wasn't proud to showcase. I began to equate my worth and value with the accomplishments of others. Other people's lives, wins, successes, and victories had become measuring devices to weigh how much my life mattered. My compass for fulfillment or success fluctuated based on the seasons of my life. When it appeared serene, quiet, and undisturbed, I exhaled in relief that somehow things were going well.

Amid everything, I suddenly became ill at work. Fear gripped me. I couldn't become sick in front of a classroom filled with children and be escorted out; so, I quietly slipped out of the classroom and headed to our school nurse. Upon checking my vitals and confirming that I had taken my daily meds, she quickly phoned my physician who instructed her to hang up and dial 911. The fear that engulfed me was unexplainable. Panic set in. What was happening to me was something beyond my control. The ambulance arrived, my vitals were retaken, a series of health questions ensued, the door was shut, and reality was the alarm clock. I was discovered, unmasked, and faced with a stark truth—I was depressed and full of anxiety. As I sat in the room with monitors blaring, calls and texts bombarding my phone, and visitors peering in to check my status, I surmised that no machine in today's technologically advanced society would denote the real underlying issue—I felt like a failure. I had no options left but to choose the path of physical and emotional healing.

My return from depression included physical check-ups, medications, and a plan to move forward. Depression had taken its toll on my body and I needed a road map to move me into fulfillment. I held true to my new regiment of meds, proper rest, and frequent doctor visits. Amid this new way of life, an opportunity arose for me to tell my story in written form. Initially, I shared with my mentor, Pastor Monica Haskell, that I didn't want to share my story. I was ashamed that the encourager needed encouraging. No one knew my diagnosis and I wasn't comfortable telling it. She assured me that my transparency and sharing my story would change lives. Indeed, writing my story on depression was therapeutic for me. Some days, the words flowed effortlessly. Other days, they were written from misted eyes. I never imagined that this stuck place would ever be a part of my purpose journey; a journey filled with twists and turns.

Rather than resent the journey, I chose to embrace it. What the devil meant for evil, God was going to turn around for my good. Part of my healing was accepting the fact that depression was a moment in my life and it didn't define me. I accepted the fact that shame was a choice and not a weight of embarrassment or a cloak worn to represent failure. I would share my story of overcoming depression with any person who would listen. As others began to hear my story, I was asked to be a speaker on different platforms (including churches) to share about overcoming depression.

Suddenly, I could see that what appeared to be designed to bury me had given way for me to birth purpose. I burst forth with joy as I began to embrace my purpose. What had been a glimmer of light in a dark place now was full of light. Brighter days indeed were lying ahead of me. I had a reason to wake up without drudgery and look forward to inspiring others to live a life designed around purpose. I began to compose a workbook designed to provoke believers to embrace their local assembly assignment and release their gifts, talents, and abilities to fortify the vision of the local church.

Harnessing the power from within, I began to step out in faith to intentionally pursue living out my life assignment— empowering others to embrace their purpose. I began sharing my story within my circle of influence to include other ministry gifts in the body. Soon, word had spread that I was the go-to person for others who were diagnosed informally or formally with symptoms of depression. With every speaking engagement, I became certain my story needed to be shared when others greeted me to share their own past or current battle with depression. To have others identify with my story and see it possible to move forward from a dark place to one filled with light and hope was exhilarating. Passion for living out my assignment began to be rekindle. I imagined the embers burning within my soul. The pain of depression had given way to a purpose assignment that fed every core of my being. Finally, I had arrived on the road named fulfillment. The light bulb went off when I became aware that fulfillment wasn't going to arrive at my front door as I had anticipated. Its form was not career, job, or people generated; it was within me all along. Its name, address, and residence were becoming known as Purpose Avenue. On this avenue, I was experiencing peace, joy, and love for life.

This in turn recharged my focus. Where the compass had previously been pointing southward, I was now heading true north—a place filled with the potential to impact and change lives daily. I began to seek God for divine connections with those who were in hot pursuit of Him and whose sole purpose was to obey Him in their assignment. This divine circle would be my designed accountability group. It would be comprised of people who embraced purpose and saw the potential of business and ministry being interrelated. Although it was difficult to see before, my eyes were wide open to the vastness of the table God was preparing for me.

It was time to connect with what I had visualized prior to that period of darkness called depression. The connection would entail building confidence, adding works with my faith, and moving strategically forward in fulfilling purpose. I had to take God at His word by following through with what was present on the canvas of my imagination. In my imagination, I saw auditoriums packed to capacity with others yearning for empowerment; eagerly waiting to gather the tools to birth their purpose and propel forward in their life assignment. In my imagination, lives were being changed at every speaking opportunity (whether in the form of a conference, workshop, or seminar setting). In my imagination, I was traveling across the globe empowering the masses to embrace the thing God created them to do. In my imagination, fulfilling my purpose was pointing others to the Creator of purpose and meeting my financial goals through serving others.

One by one, God started connecting the dots. I could see the missing puzzle pieces interlocking and the purpose-filled picture of my life coming closer into view. It was time to develop an action plan to move forward in purpose. That plan included moving beyond fear and hosting my own live events centered around inspiring others to embrace their purpose. I strategically set out to relaunch a Facebook community to empower others daily in their purpose. The relaunch was a direct result of one of my accountability partners, Minister Rebecca D. Huggins, emphatically saying, "Do it." Fear was trying to choke the breath out of me and discount my faith. These were waters I had treaded before but hadn't reached the shores of growth or engagement within the community. I reevaluated who the community was designed to serve.

Obeying God on the other side of depression would lead to me not only birthing purpose but being Souled Out to God. It was time to celebrate His goodness and faithfulness for never leaving or forsaking me amid the darkest period of my life. It was time to allow myself the boldness I had coached many others to unlock in their pursuit of showing up for God. I saw another person begin to emerge from behind an invisible cloak of darkness. She was bold, she was confident, she was ready (although trusting and trembling) to move into an element of uncertainty that would include new, unchartered territories. I committed to show up every day; showcasing purpose in varying ways and platforms. I garnered enough confidence to begin recording purpose-filled messages while out on my daily walk. Others began to share, comment, or like the videos, but the fuel was seeing myself stick with my personal vow to show up regularly by sharing the message of embracing your purpose. The goal became crystal clear: it was necessary to model and demonstrate the thing God was requiring of us all as believers, which was to live out our purpose assignment; one that would give Him glory and benefit others. Day by day, I saw this purpose video message provoking others to embrace their own purpose. Passion became fuel to propel me forward, gaining momentum for future projects. Scheduling a calendar of events to change lives became doable, desired, and paramount to my destiny. What my soul had yearned for the most was swiftly coming to pass—a life Souled Out to the One who had redeemed me from sudden destruction, replaced darkness with light, turned my mourning into dancing, and my sorrow into joy.

Living in the Presence of God

SHIRLEY JEAN BAZEMORE

*"But those who hope in the Lord will renew their strength.
They will soar on wings like eagles; they will run and
not grow weary, they will walk and not be faint."*

Isaiah 40:31 (NIV)

When was the last time you asked yourself, "Is it my time to soar?" Do not put it off until tomorrow when God has already told you to soar like an eagle. An eagle is big; therefore, you must have big dreams, visions, and goals. You must set your mind to the greatest opportunities in life.

Living in the presence of God will prepare you to see endeavors more clearly.

My morning begins with "The Lord's Prayer":

"Our Father in heaven, hallowed be your name, your kingdom come, your will be done, on earth as it is in heaven. Give us today our daily bread. And forgive us our debts, as we also have forgiven our debtors. And lead us not into temptation, but deliver us from the evil one" (Matthew 6:9-13 NIV). Good morning, Father. Good morning, Holy Spirit. What are we going to do today? I ask to be blessed, so I can be a blessing to others. I ask for wisdom on today."

Your prayer life is an important part of your day. In your place of prayer, you will get assignments for the day.

"God's word provides us with hope, even in our darkest hour, though we may not always see it," stated Dr. Benjamin Mast.

My darkest hour came when I received the phone call from my doctor. "Ms. Bazemore, I am calling you with the results of your lab work. You are a diabetic and have rheumatoid arthritis. We have to schedule you to see a specialist for your rheumatoid arthritis."

As a believer, I received the information, but did not put too much emphasis on it. I was too busy working at the time, because my job was very demanding. I was focused on my job and meeting my deadlines.

I realized how serious my health was when my knee gave out while I was at work. I was standing in the hallway talking with a coworker and I just went to the floor. My coworker was in total shock.

African-Americans and Diabetes

The rate of diabetes in blacks has tripled over the past 30 years. Diagnosed diabetes in adults is now 1.4 times as frequent in blacks as in whites. This excess occurs for both black men and black women. According to the American Diabetes Association, approximately 1.3 million African-Americans have been diagnosed as having diabetes.

Type 2 diabetes: Your body does not use insulin properly. This is called insulin resistance. The pancreas makes extra insulin to make up for it. Your pancreas is not able to keep up and cannot make enough insulin to keep your blood glucose levels normal. When glucose builds up in the blood instead of going into cells, it can cause two problems: (1) Right away your cells may be starved for energy, (2) Over time high blood glucose levels may hurt your eyes, kidneys, nerves or heart. Type 2 diabetes is more common in African-Americans.

Symptoms of Diabetes in Both Women and Men:
1. Excessive hunger or thirst (dry mouth)
2. Fatigue
3. Frequent urination
4. Cuts and wounds that heal slowly
5. Recurrent chest/urinary infections
6. Unexplained weight loss
7. Blurred vision
8. Headaches
9. Reduced sensation in hands and feet
10. Recurring skin infections

Understanding Rheumatoid Arthritis

Since being diagnosed with rheumatoid arthritis, my life has changed dramatically. The activities I once enjoyed become obsolete because of the excruciating pain.

Rheumatoid arthritis is an incurable, inflammatory, autoimmune disorder in which the body's immune system attacks its own healthy tissues for reasons that are poorly understood. RA is most closely associated with potentially disabling destruction and deformation of the joints, but it is characterized by widespread inflammation that attacks multiple organ systems throughout the body, including the heart, lungs, blood vessels, eyes, and skin.

This inflammation is caused by elevated levels of several proteins, called cytokines, found in the blood, including tumor necrosis factor alpha, interleukin-1, and interleukin-6. The cytokines may also promote cognitive impairment through a variety of mechanisms (Arthritis Foundation/Rheumatoid Arthritis.net Treatment-WebMD).

According to Dr. Mark Swain, a professor of medicine and Head of the Division of Gastroenterology at the University of Calgary, people often complain of brain fog. Studies suggest that 30 to 70 percent of RA patients have cognitive impairment. Brain fog is a widely used, nonmedical term that is often applied to describe a person's inability to think clearly, remember things, concentrate, or easily carry out day-to-day tasks. Living with RA and having brain fog, you might ask yourself questions like, "why did I come into this room?" Or you could have trouble recalling names, appointments, birthdays, or important dates. You may even find it difficult to remember how to perform routine tasks at work, and could have a tough time making simples decisions. Experiencing brain fog can be traumatic.

Although there is not yet a cure for rheumatoid arthritis, early treatment has been shown to help to prevent disability. About 1.3 million American adults (more women than men) have RA. Also, women did not respond as well as men to the same treatment.

Living in the presence of God is the true release I have in my life. Your RA treatments are just temporary. You have some of the best doctors, but the treatments affect everyone differently. You encounter the side effects from the medicine. When we are faced with trials, tribulations, and health challenges, we ask, "God, why me?" I asked over and over again, "Why me?" I have been one of the caregivers for my mother and father, but now I am in a situation where I need to depend on someone else for help. I had to swallow my pride and ask for help.

I have always been an independent person, but for a couple of months I had to rely on family and friends to help. God always had my friend and neighbor, Randy, there for support. God places people in our lives to help out, and they probably do understand why they are there for you.

The Renewing of Your Mind

I was living in silence with my pain because it was affecting my body. My body was changing right in front of my eyes, and I could do nothing but pray and pray. When people saw me, they had no idea of the chronic pain I was living with because I was smiling on the outside and suffering in silence.

The more I lived in the presence of God, Satan attacked even stronger. I had other friends who were facing health challenges, so I was trying to be strong and pray for them. I was keeping my suffering silent and talking to God more and more. Living in the presence of God, my TV time was no longer important. I went from spending 30 minutes in the presence of God to spending hours in His presence.

When death came knocking at my door the first time, I said, "No. No weapon formed against me shall prosper. I bind and rebuke you in the name of Jesus."

When death came knocking at my door the second time I said, "No, I plead the blood of Jesus. I bind and rebuke you in the name of Jesus."

When death came knocking at my door the third time I said, "No. Why don't you give up? You have no power here. I have the power to trample over you in the name of Jesus." I had my family's love and support every time. When a challenge comes your way, open the door and say, "Mr. Challenge, I was not expecting you so soon. But, now that you are here, come on in. God already told me just what to do, and exactly how to deal with you today."

Pray Ephesians 6:10-18 (NIV)

"Finally, be strong in the Lord and in his mighty power. Put on the full armor of God, so that you can take your stand against the devil's schemes. For our struggle is not against flesh and blood, but against the rulers, against the authorities, against the powers of this dark world and against the spiritual forces of evil in the heavenly realms. Therefore put on the full armor of God, so that when the day of evil comes, you may be able to stand your ground, and after you have done everything, to stand. Stand firm then, with the belt of truth buckled around your waist, with the breastplate of righteousness in place, and with your feet fitted with the readiness that comes from the gospel of peace. In addition to all this, take up the shield of faith, with which you can extinguish all the flaming arrows of the evil one. Take the helmet of salvation and the sword of the Spirit, which is the word of God. And pray in the Spirit on all occasions with all kinds of prayers and requests. With this in mind, be alert and always keep on praying for all the Lord's people."

Having a Conversation with the Holy Spirit

As I spent more time in God's presence, He began connecting me with powerful and anointed prayer warriors. After finishing "The Psalms Challenge" with Bonita, I was put in Cheryl's path. Then, I met April in KCC Church. Being in a good Bible-based church is important too. She introduced me to "The 120 Journey" prayer line. I met my spiritual mothers, Apostle Phelps and Apostle Jones. I also met Sister Rosemary and a lot of powerful intercessory prayer warriors. Then, I met Prophetess Johnson. Living in the presence of God often starts at 3:00 a.m. by giving God thanks and listening to His instructions.

Conversation with God at 3:00 a.m.:

Holy Spirit: "Wake up."
Me: "God, I am tired and sleepy."
Holy Spirit: "We need to talk."
Me: "Why? Why?"
Holy Spirit: "Repent and pray."
Me: "I am praying and asking for forgiveness."
Holy Spirit: "I need for you to pray about this situation."

Me:	"God, I have been praying a lot for other people."
Holy Spirit:	"Yes, that's why I need for you to stay in my presence."
Me:	"God, I need prayer too. Who's praying for me?"
Holy Spirit:	"You already know people are covering you in prayer every day."
Me:	"Yes, thank you for everyone praying for me. I need all the prayer I can get."
Holy Spirit:	"After you pray, read a chapter from (book), and meditate on what you read."
Me:	"The study begins 3:00 a.m. in the morning."
Holy Spirit:	"In the morning, these are things you need to do, etc."

After I have finished my time with God, I begin giving Him praise and thanks for everything. So, when you cannot sleep at night, God is trying to tell you something. God wants to align your thoughts with His thoughts. He is preparing you to be a greater person. God wants to see His glory inside of you. He wants to know if you are willing to do His will and be obedient to His Word. God is checking your faith to see how strong it is. "For we walk by faith, not by sight" (2 Corinthians 5:7 ESV).

The Word for the Day:
When the Holy Spirit lays something on your heart, move without hesitation. You have no idea who may be depending on your immediate obedience. When we sense an internal

witness encouraging us to take a certain course of action, we should listen. The Holy Spirit always guides you to understand and accept the Father's will. He is the One speaking to your heart, warning you about danger, and encouraging you to submit to God's purposes. In John 14:26 ESV, Jesus promised us: "But the Helper, the Holy Spirit, whom the Father will send in my name, he will teach you all things."

My Declaration:
I AM who God says I AM
I AM who the Bible says I AM
A child of God, A branch of the true vines
I have been justified and redeemed so I fear no one; I will not be condemned by God
I AM righteous and sanctified. God will always lead me to triumph!
I AM an heir of the kingdom
I AM a citizen of Heaven
God will supply all my needs
I AM successful
I AM bearing fruits
I AM gifted
I AM God's Daughter

Souled Out Reflection:
(S)hirley, (O)bedience, (U)nderstanding, (L)ove, (E)xternal, (D)evoted–(O)ne, (U)niverse, (T)estimony: Do not lose heart, Shirley. "Though outwardly we are wasting away, yet inwardly we are being renewed day by day. For our light and momentary troubles are achieving for us an eternal glory

that far outweighs them all. So we fix our eyes not on what is seen, but on what is unseen, since what is seen is temporary, but what is unseen is eternal" (2 Corinthians 4:16-18 NIV).

Dysfunctional Loyalty

DR. HELENA V. HILL

*"Those who don't know the value of loyalty, can
never appreciate the cost of betrayal."*

—Unknown

I'm Dr. Helena V. Hill, a senior pastor, wife, mother, grandmother, award-winning author, certified life coach, inspirational speaker, and entrepreneur. As you can see, I wear
several hats. I assure you they aren't all worn simultane-
ously. You can say at times that life requests for me to stack
my hats high. I will be bold enough to say that you may also
be wearing several hats at this time. In that case, we have
just bonded.

As a woman of several hats, I realized balance is
necessary to get the assignments of God completed, while
keeping in mind that my first assignment is to minister to my
home and to keep it maintained. Although you do have God
in your life, it can be a challenge to manage it all at once. I
would like to share a challenge I had in my life, during which
I felt like I was losing it.

My challenge stemmed from the poor choices I made in my life. Those choices placed me in a temporary prison. I was young and inexperienced, with little exposure to personality types or behavioral and spiritual signs toward dysfunctional traits. These limitations marked me as prey for those who crafted themselves as experts of manipulation in the church. These people look for our type: loyal, dedicated, naïve, trustworthy, protectors who are looking to belong. If this description fits you, I pray this chapter will prevent you from entering a situation, or help you get out of or recover from a situation.

I would like to make sure that first we are defining our topic from the same perspective. My definition of dysfunctional is: having an unhealthy, abnormal behavior or attitude toward others. Loyalty is: being faithful to commitments and obligations. I want to point out that there is nothing wrong with being a loyal person. The opposing questions are: What are you being loyal to? Is what you are giving your loyalty to also loyal?

I gave my loyalty to a young evangelist several years ago. At the time, I was separated and seven months pregnant. I had moved back home into a one-bedroom apartment with my oldest son who was one. I was on the system, going to school, and coping with a complicated pregnancy. I would remind myself, from time to time, of the Word according to Proverbs 3:5-6, "Trust in the LORD with all your heart and lean not on your own understanding; in all your ways submit to him, and he will make your paths straight" (NIV). This Scripture would help soothe me during this time. Do you have a Scripture that helps soothe your heart and mind as you are dealing with your situation?

I recall my first conversation with the young evangelist through my screen door. There was no hospitality shown besides the value of my time to hear him. The young evangelist shared his desire for me to take my kids' dad back. Of course, I immediately rejected the idea of having him back in my life.

After a while, I decided to visit the church where the young evangelist assisted and my kids' dad attended. The evangelist was speaking during this occasion and I enjoyed the message. We began to develop a brother-sister relationship. I did eventually allow my kids' dad to come back into my life.

The young evangelist announced to the pastor that he was led by God to begin his own ministry. I was not a member of the other church, so I had no problem with following him. I had not fully developed the spirit of discernment. God was giving me a warning, but I did not take heed. Being young and strong-willed, I made the mistake many have made when you move in self; I did not pray and seek God's face concerning becoming a part of that church. I did not apply the Word according to Matthew 7:15, "Beware of false prophets who come disguised as harmless sheep but are really vicious wolves" (NLT). Have you ever made a decision without consulting God?

Things started out good... so I thought. I noticed a change coming over him. He eventually married and began to have children. He wasn't the person I thought I knew. He would share private conversations he had in counseling over the pulpit. He would instigate situations that would cause discord in the families and within the church. I knew church was not to be conducted in this manner. Instead of speaking with him, I would rationalize this behavior due to his lack of maturity in leadership. Yes, I prayed but it was for his maturity not for discernment. I had not yet applied the Scripture, 1 John 4:1, "Dear friends, do not believe every spirit, but test the spirits to see whether they are from God, because many false prophets have gone out into the world" (NIV).

Sadly, those previous episodes were just the introduction to what was to come. He would be exceptionally kind to newcomers. He would do special things for them. He would take excessive time out with them. After he went so far, he would begin to call in what he had done. He would make them feel guilty and obligated to him. He would call them out of their names over the pulpit. The same people he had uplifted. This strategy is called manipulation. He would make the statement, "After all I did for you." He would tell others what he did. Beware of this kind of getting to know or befriend you method. It has a deep effect on your emotions. Here are two familiar repercussions: 1) If I need something from you and you do not comply, there will be repercussions. 2) If you don't do something for me when I ask, there will be repercussions. Beware if a person can get you to feel obligated to the point that you reduce or negate your spiritual, ethical, and moral values. They have you almost where they want you. I would like for you to evaluate your current relationships. Make sure they are healthy.

As time progressed, I realized I did not want to see the wrong. I just wanted to see the person I knew back then. The person who I thought was genuine. The person I thought cared about me and my family. The person I thought only wanted to do things God's way. I finally realized I was witnessing a Jim Jones movement. My prayer had evolved to, "God, help him to want to change to do things your way." My loyalty said, "He really doesn't mean to hurt people to this degree. He has a lot on him." As you can see, I was making excuses for bipolar, narcissistic, and schizophrenic behavior. The Word according to Matthew 23:3 says, "So you must be careful to do everything they tell you. But do not do what they do, for they do not practice what they preach" (NIV).

The dysfunctional behavior escalated to dictating to the members whether or not they could spend time with their families, if they could further their education, and taking the church money to spend it on whatever he wanted although the church was giving him a nice weekly salary. He would manipulate members who had money for his gain. He would use various Scriptures, an attitude, and threats of leaving the city to get the people to give more money. He would talk about how he didn't owe anyone anything when the people had a need and the ministry could not help them because he spent over the budget. The Word according to 1 Timothy 3:3 says, "... not violent but gentle, not quarrelsome, not a lover of money" (NIV).

You would have thought that was enough for me; but no, it wasn't. The negative trait of a loyal person is that we will stay in a situation far too long because we want to see the manifestation of the change for which we've prayed. The finale was when my family and I were put out of the ministry after 21 years of service because he changed his mind about my ministry assignment. As an adult, of course a meeting to discuss the sudden change would be natural; instead, he chose to share the private conversation (that I thought went well) over the pulpit as the sermon for the morning. God had instructed me on what to do before going to service. He let me know this was the day I would shake the dust off my feet and never return. The Word according to Matthew 10:14 says, "If anyone will not welcome you or listen to your words, leave that home or town and shake the dust off your feet" (NIV).

You may find yourself in one or more of these scenarios of dysfunctional behavior. I used the church experience because many people are dealing with these typical issues. They are left feeling like they are wrong because they believe the things they witness or are asked to do are not of God. You are correct. It is not of God for you to be treated in this manner. You can, and should, be loyal to the ministry of the Gospel and the Shepherd without being abused spiritually, mentally, physically, and financially.

What I want to point out now are the basic dysfunctional signs to look for in your relationships, whether spiritual, personal or business. Note that these are only a few signs to look for:

1.   Emotional blocks: I view this as the ultimate warning sign. When fear, jealousy, obsession, non-involvement, manipulation, distrust, suspicion, disrespect, and an uncaring attitude are displayed as the norm of your relationship, you should be concerned. When you notice that someone else's ways are controlling your emotions or that you are doing the controlling, you've created an unhealthy relationship.

2. Constant unhappiness: I know this is simple, but your happiness matters. Periodically, you need to ask yourself these questions: Am I happy? If not, what happened? Am I continuously unhappy and feeling mentally bogged down because something is wrong? This happens when you or your partner cannot rectify your feelings, needs, and desires.

3. Inferiority/Superiority complex: A strong concern for your relationship should arise when it turns into a comparison. You are not in competition with your partner. A healthy relationship has equal efforts and opinions that bring the necessary contributions of balance.

4. Being unsure and insecure: This is a concern when you go from being a spontaneous person to being overcautious about doing things you would normally do without a second thought. If you are unsure you will become insecure. Watch for the change in yourself or your partner's confidence.

5. The feeling of frustration: This is when frustration never really subsides. Do not ignore this behavior. There is something wrong.

6. Addictive/Obsessive attitude: This is when you or your partner develops an addictive or obsessive attitude. Your focus is abnormally on yourself or your partner. Many may consider your action obsession. Caution, this is the beginning of dysfunctional.

7. Tension shows up regularly: You find that minor issues cause great tension in your home. Things

like work, family, friends, and money may enhance the tension, positioning these areas as priority issues.

8. Imbalance of power: This is when you feel as though you are working much harder than your partner is on your relationship. The example of your effort is a 90/10 ratio, reflecting that one of you is working more than the other. This relationship is going toward the dysfunctional stage.

9. Feeling cornered: This is when you or your partner develops a feeling of being cornered or trapped in a situation neither of you would have originally entered. If these feelings repeatedly occur, it may be a sign that there could potentially be a problem.

For your convenience, here is the link to an online healthy relationship assessment test. It is important to know if you are in a healthy relationship. www.loveisrespect.org/for-someone-else/is-my-relationship-healthy-quiz/

I want you to develop healthy relationships. As a loyal person, I tended to rationalize—using explanations instead of looking for solutions. The longer I kept my mouth closed, I formulated explanation after explanation for abnormal behavior, not realizing I was moving toward a dysfunctional mindset. You can get lost in chaos. The longer you position yourself in a situation that reduces your character, disposition, integrity, and confidence you will become comfortable with an unhealthy situation. You will focus on pleasing the other person. Now, you are losing yourself. Remind yourself of Galatians 1:10, "Am I now trying to win the approval of human beings, or of God? Or am I trying to please people? If I were still trying to please people, I would not be a servant of Christ" (NIV). You can lose yourself in a dysfunctional relationship.

The only way I could come out of the progressive prison was by doing one major thing along with prayer. I took time to step away from the situation. I had to stop rationalizing. I began to view my situation from the outside instead of from the inside. I found out that as long as I was inside of the situation, I would never see it from a different perspective. I had to get my mind recalibrated from all the years of continuous abuse. I had to get back every valuable thing that was stripped away, and some things that I offered. I had to get my confidence back. I had to tell myself I was not wrong about the truth I knew. I had to accept that there would be retaliation for my stand. I had to break the controlling spirit in the form of manipulation. I had to affirm within myself that no one should have that much influence over your emotions to the point that it alters your thinking. I had to regain my identity. I had to pray for direction to get out of the situation. I had to do it God's way not mine. I am blessed to say that I was able to get out of the situation with my right mind. The scars I accumulated have healed with time. It was a gradual process, but it was worth it. I had to get professional and spiritual counseling. That is why I can talk to you today. My passion is to help others who may be entering, are in, or are coming out of a dysfunctional relationship by sharing my story, the nine signs of dysfunctional behavior, and an online assessment. Many of us have experienced at least one dysfunctional relationship. I am a survivor. Are you next?

Love Is the Key

CYNDE JOY

"Let my life be the proof,
The proof of Your love"

Song lyrics by: for KING & COUNTRY

"Let all that you do be done in love."

1 Corinthians 16:14 (ESV)

I was in and out of foster care or on the streets during my teenage years. I learned quickly that this was a big, scary world and I felt like I was alone, unprotected. I saw everything as either good or bad. To my understanding, there were no dimensions. I was safe or I was at risk of losing my life. I didn't know there was a different way. I didn't know God was with me; always loving me even before I loved Him. Having experienced this as a teenager, I had a desire to foster teenage girls. Before finding Jesus and a path to freedom from my past, I spent many of my adult years going through many trials, including abuse and homelessness. Now, I could serve the Lord by ministering to others as He put them in my path. The thought of a child out in the world all alone needing a safe place to land and someone to love them became a passionate, growing concern of mine. I had raised all but one of my biological children, who was now a teenager, and she was all in on this. I was a single mom most of those years and am single now. On some small level, I knew this would be difficult; but, I really had no idea how difficult. The only way to foster these kids was going to be through God leading the way with His strength, love, and wisdom. My own strength wasn't going to be sufficient.

I prayed, asking for God's will and guidance for fostering to come to fruition. My house was too small for this venture, so I stepped out in faith with a wonderful friend who helped me to fix up my house. I bought it for a great price 15 years prior, and I was amazed when I was offered almost $10,000.00 more than my asking price. God is so good. After I sold my house, I started looking for what God would bless me to share with the girls that would come. I looked at houses and was feeling disappointed about what I saw in my price range. I was about to give up when my real estate agent asked if I would consider moving to a town nearby. I figured it wouldn't hurt to look. We walked into a house and I was stunned. I told her to bid on it before we left. There was a lot of competition. I was very surprised when I got the call that I'd won the bid. I remembered looking at similar houses when I was homeless and living in rundown shacks. I thought, "How do people make enough money to buy and live in a house like that?" I had no clue then; yet, here I was years later buying one. When God gives you a vision for a mission, He will provide the means. Soon after I bought the house, I heard an advertisement on the radio about foster care. I called them and started the process of becoming a licensed foster care provider. It took a year of preparation. I did fire and safety inspections, home studies, installed safety measures around the house, and took classes. I bought furniture and bedding for the foster girls that would come. Finally, I was approved and handed my license for my foster home. The license read: "Treatment Level Foster Home." I had no idea all the classes I took along with degrees I had earned and my work experience had qualified me for this.

I was handed a checklist. Will you take a child who is aggressive, sets fires, is cruel to animals, has suicidal ideation, and more? Oh, Lord, I hadn't anticipated those issues. I prayed more. "God, please send me the children you want me to help." I checked off what I felt I could handle and marked off what I thought was too much for me. I looked and prayed over what they call a Common Core Application to pick a child I would like to accept into my home. They sent me everything. The checklist was ignored. I finally found an application, for a 14-year-old young lady, who I felt comfortable saying yes to. She was living in a shelter and had some rough bumps in the road, but was not a danger for burning the house down or stabbing me in my sleep. They contacted the caseworker and then came back with a counteroffer. Her 12-year-old sister was not doing well in her current foster home and I was asked to consider reuniting the girls in my home. Absolutely! I was so excited. My daughter and I went shopping to make welcome gifts for the girl's beds, got them stuffed animals because we both still liked stuffed animals, and then waited patiently for them to arrive. The day finally arrived, and both the agency and CPS caseworkers brought the girls to my house. The girls jumped out of the cars and ran to hug each other while smiling, talking, crying, and laughing, then they came up the walkway. The older one walked up to me and hugged me. She looked at me and said, "Thank you for taking my sister and I when no one else would." My heart was so touched, I had to compose myself for a minute. We signed papers and they found the bedroom and presents. Then, the caseworkers said, "Okay, see you later," and they left. I was speechless. I knew they were bringing me children and would leave them with me, but when they did I was momentarily frozen in my steps. They trusted me with real live children. They gave them to me and left.

There were two weeks of what I learned is called "The Honeymoon Stage." It was lovely. Then came the storms of their lives pouring out and darkening all the crevices of our home. Where there was once light and joy, the darkness was moving in. When I bought my home, I prayed over the actual structure of the house. I asked for blessings and prayed that I would be a good steward of what I had received. Now, I went back and prayed against all principalities, and spiritual, mental, and emotional attacks being waged against all of us. "For our struggle is not against flesh and blood, but against the rulers, against the authorities, against the powers of this dark world and against the spiritual forces of evil in the heavenly realms" (Ephesians 6:12 NIV).

Teenagers are cantankerous, rebellious souls even when life has been stable and full of love. It is a normal thing for them to have growing pains while they find out who they are and what they want to be. Foster children have experienced abuse and or neglect at some level, enough to be taken away from their family; yet, no matter the danger and dysfunction, they love that family unconditionally. These children grieve the loss of their families. They grieve hard. They are broken children that rightfully are too immature to cope with all the change, confusion and loss. On top of all the loss and grief, the foster care system is broken as well. This makes things even worse. By the time my foster children came to me, they had been in many homes and shelters. They had met good, caring people and people just doing their job. They didn't trust anyone and didn't want to bond with anyone else that would give up and make them move on. The issues that came with the children were big. Many of the things I identified as can't do on the list manifested in these children. One of those issues were suicidal ideation and attempts. This hit a very raw nerve for me. One of my own children had attempted suicide multiple times during her teen years. Now as an adult, she had overcome and become an amazing young woman. But my ex-husband had successfully completed suicide and all of that had been hard; so, I was no stranger to it, but I didn't want to face it again on a personal level. These times were times spent on my knees crying out to God to calm my heart and anxiety. I cried out to God to help me help them. Some of the problems were big; there were psychiatric hospital visits and residential treatment stays. The other child felt angry, anxious, and trapped. She yelled in my face and tried hard to get me to join her in her personal chaos. It was the only way she felt comfortable. Drama was her comfort lifestyle. She knew what to expect from that. Another child came to stay with us. She was so sweet when she was sweet, but so violent when she was mad. I could not take care of her on my own. I had to supervise her every minute. She tore up the church one day during services. I have an awesome church. The men helped me contain her while the pastor kept preaching. We locked down the nursery area and got her in my car, but she hopped out and ran back in to wreak more havoc. We finally called the police. I called the church to apologize to my pastor and tell him the plan I had, so that if we could come back that wouldn't happen again. You know what he said? "We love you and support you in this ministry. We love these broken children with you. You are more worried about this than we are. Bring her back and let us love her some more with you." Wow! God is so good to have provided such a church family as this to love these precious children with me. Eventually, I had to let go and let God work with her in a facility. I do continue to support her, and I visit her where she is safe to get the help she needs. I wanted her to know she was loved and not rejected by yet another person. I wanted her to know I cared enough to get her what she needed.

I got a phone call one day that brought three small children with emotional and special needs to my home for the summer, which became a yearlong struggle. They were loud, strong- willed, destructive, and broken. They were also small, cute, full of energy, and always curious about something. They had interesting questions about death and God, and a real need to connect to Him. One of them noticed a prayer was answered before I did. She said, "Ms. Cynde, did you see? We prayed, and the phone rang, and the person answered our prayer." I paused and realized I would have missed that moment. A moment that built both our faiths.

What I did start to see in myself was me working hard for these children. Me thinking through each problem and using my experience and education to come up with plans to make differences. And we did make progress. The youngest who was nonverbal became very verbal. Whew, you should not have heard some of the words that came out of that baby's mouth. They went from anger to times of smiles and giggles, but in my own strength I was wearing thin. I was breaking down. My blood pressure was going up, my tolerance was going down, and I was falling short. We all fall short of the glory of God and sin. I was getting angry and taking things personally when I knew better. I knew it was not about me. I was just there in the combat zone and I was taking hits. My armor was getting chipped away. Previously, I had calmly addressed issues and assaults as they came, now I was becoming anxious and occasionally yelling back to be heard. A caseworker said to me, "You had the grace for this job, but it is gone. Maybe it is time to quit. No one will blame you. These kids are difficult." I was tired. I crawled into my bathroom where I prayed and questioned God. "I know You called me to this, but I am not doing this in excellence for You. In fact, I am falling, and this is getting bad. I need help. I am a professional and parented my own children successfully, but I am failing here. What am I doing wrong?" I heard God say to my spirit, "You are tired because YOU are doing this in your own strength. This is a hard job. This is a God job not a Cynde job. I am your strength. All I called you to do is love these children and be an example to them. Walk in obedience to me and I will do the work."

The great I AM will make the difference. You are called to pour into these children with love, time, and sacrifice. Plant the seeds of love and faith, but know that God is the heart changer. And just as He was changing my heart and growing me, He is faithful to be the heart changer for all these precious children too. He loves them the most. I was to be His hands to hold and guide their hands, His arms to wrap them up in big hugs of safe love, and His feet to walk them through the dark valleys to the light-filled mountain tops. So, I got up and looked in the mirror, pointed my finger in my face, and told myself, "This is not about you. Step out of the way and step into the game. Be all in and do it in the spirit of God."

Soulful Reflection:

I must remind myself to drop to my knees daily. I must look in the mirror and encourage myself with a smile to follow Him or reprimand myself because this is not about me. This is for His glory, for His children that He has given into my care to steward with love. It can be a never-ending story full of hope—the one where love begets more love and service, as we all grow in Christ.

"May the God of hope fill you with all joy and peace as you trust in him, so that you may overflow with hope by the power of the Holy Spirit."

Romans 15:13 (NIV)

My Struggles Became His Strategy for My Strength

ROBIN HAIR

"As for you, you meant evil against me, but God meant it for good in order to bring about this present result, to preserve many people alive."

Genesis 50:20 (NASB)

My world fell apart with one phone call from the other woman. Now, I am laying on the floor in my brother's spare bedroom with my two children asleep next to me. It's the middle of the night and I am wide awake in shock wondering, "How did I get here?"

Introducing the Nightmare on Elm Street movie starring Robin Hair! In the story, characters fall asleep and have nightmares of trying to escape a mutilated villain with knives for fingers who is taunting them and threatening to take their lives and their sanity. Anyone he kills in the dream, dies in real life. Wake up before he gets you! You finally regain consciousness only to realize your nightmare is just beginning! You are still asleep! Keep running!

My first nightmare lasted 16 years. Tormented by mental abuse, infidelity and adultery, financial instability, and betrayal, I so desperately wanted to wake up! I thought I had done everything possible to strategically position myself for success in life. I wanted the dream of a beautiful home, successful career, and to celebrate a silver wedding anniversary of 50 years someday with a family who was dedicated to serving Christ. Nothing was further from the truth.

I was born in Philadelphia, Pennsylvania. My mother was an amazing tower of strength who gave me a legacy of hard work and tenacity. She was a single mother raising three children: me and my two brothers. I was the baby of the family. We had a large extended family who always got together for holidays, barbecues, and block parties. Even though I come from a lineage of Baptist preachers, we did not go to church often except for Easter, Christmas, and Vacation Bible School. We moved to Savannah, Georgia, for my mom to take care of my grandparents.

Savannah is such a beautiful place with lots of great memories. I attended Sol C. Johnson High School. I was very outgoing and a high achiever. I was captain of the drill team and flag corp. I was awarded a scholarship to attend Savannah State University where I earned my Bachelor of Arts Degree in Marketing. In college, I was captain of the cheerleaders, and I pledged Alpha Kappa Alpha, Sorority Inc. as well as Delta Sigma Pi Professional Business Fraternity. Later in life, I earned my MBA from the Savannah Campus of University of Phoenix. I was equipped for success... or so I thought. After graduating from Savannah State University with honors, I was offered an opportunity to move to Indianapolis, Indiana, to work for IBM as a Marketing Representative.

Now, this is where my nightmare begins at age 25; when I agree to marry Judas—a man who had a history of infidelity, deception, instability, and adultery. Shortly after I got married, I met Jesus. Jesus and I had a long-lasting, intimate, unbreakable bond and relationship. Judas and I did not. Years later, fed up, I decided to relocate to Atlanta, Georgia, to get away from his girlfriend's taunting phone calls at home and at work. Promising to change, he went with me and so did the problem.

Jesus was my joy and my peace during this storm. Now, here is a huge lesson: ignorance (naïveté) is not an excuse. God warns not to be yoked together with unbelievers. "For what do righteousness and wickedness have in common? Or what fellowship can light have with darkness?" (2 Corinthians 6:14 NIV). Please understand that having a relationship with Christ does not make you immune to the consequences of foolish decisions. While God's grace and mercy endures forever, God will not take control of your unrelenting spouse or boyfriend to make them do the right thing if they do not want Him to. Pray, fast, and anoint the whole house with oil. Roll around on his side of the bed speaking in tongues and all of that. Go all out. Pour blessed oil in all his shoes and on the pillow. Seek counseling. That is what a wife is supposed to do in a situation like mine. I believe God is a miracle working God. He is truly able. Countless stories of how the husband gave his life to Christ due to the relentless prayers and example of the wife motivated me; however, this never became my story. Spiritually, I had grown tremendously. After we became Hope Ministers, God told me, "I will show you that your husband is not going to change.

So now that you know the truth, what are you going to do?" Hence the phone call from that woman which changed everything. I left.

A worse dream was just beginning. I move back home to Savannah from Atlanta and now I am trying to console my two children whose worlds have been ripped apart due to the divorce. I lost everything: house, car, income, etc. I applied for food stamps and stood in line at The Salvation Army, wearing my business suit, to get toys for my children. Who does that? Through it all, I never left God. I immediately found a new church, got a job, eventually bought another house, and connected with the community. I did not really let God deal with what I was going through. For three years, I saw myself as the victim. I crammed my schedule with all kinds of activity involving the children, the community, and my church; trying to prove to myself and others that I had a lot to offer somebody if only they would see it. I stayed so busy, I did not reflect on the hard truth of my life. I was not awake. I was still asleep and living in denial, which is a different kind of torment. I had buried the pain.

This nightmare switches to a different scene and a different Judas shows up. This time, I start believing a whole other set of lies. He painted the picture of a glamorous life. He promises he is a Godly man. He has plans to build million-dollar businesses. I saw the business plans, and he told me that as his wife I didn't have to work. We joined the local country club. We hobnobbed with the local celebrities. I saw the money coming in. He surprised me with a champagne colored Avalon and told me I would never have to make a payment. What he didn't tell me was he was never going to make a payment either! He was sleeping with other women for money. But, I was responsible. Why? Because I wanted to believe the lies. They sounded good. I ignored the initial warning signs of a career con-man. Now, I couldn't work because I had a bleeding disorder. He said he would take care of all the bills, but we had no health insurance. I was slowly dying. Jesus worked through a community health facility, and I got the surgery I needed.

As I was recovering and getting my strength back, I noticed that all the bills were behind. I started getting foreclosure notices and repossession warnings for the Avalon. Bills that he had created came flooding in with my name on them. When I confronted him, he left, and I never saw him again. That nightmare lasted 18 months. The aftermath was more devastating than the first divorce. It was a nuclear fallout. Hit men came knocking on my door looking for him, so I hid from them. The police showed up at my door looking for him. Even though I had the locks changed, I did not feel safe; so, I left the house and moved into an apartment. I found myself in court because my name was tied to his. Again, I lost my house, the Avalon, and my good name. I was bankrupt. I had to ride my daughter's bike to pay bills or walk to look for work. Neighbors took me to the store. I found myself with two degrees, working overnight at the front desk of a hotel. I had gone from making $70,000.00 per year to $8.50 an hour working the graveyard shift, and my wages were garnished! I thank God for family and friends who helped me through this horrible time. How could a saved, sanctified, filled with the Holy Ghost, speaking in unknown tongues, educated, professional businesswoman end up in this mess again? I was so embarrassed that I never talked about my second marriage until this book. I hope this transparency will help somebody get free.

How was I going to wake up? I had to get to know my greatest advocate: Jesus Christ. I noticed that each time I focused on Jesus and took my eyes off my desires, my plans, and my demands, the results were amazing revelations and clarity. My problem was listening to only part of God's revelation. He revealed the truth in each of my situations when I sat still long enough to listen; however, I only had part of the truth and didn't wait for instructions. I just ran with it without consulting Him for my next move. I would tell God what I wanted Him to do instead of asking Him what He wanted me to do. My mind, will, and emotions were running my life. My soul needed to be reborn.

Get to know Jesus so He can tell you who you are. I did not know myself. He knows us better than we know ourselves. Everything you think, say, do, pray, and believe sends a message to the universe to manifest those things in your life whether they be good, bad, ugly, or indifferent. But the enemy is also watching and waiting to use our weaknesses and ignorance against us. He masquerades as an answer to our prayers.

The nightmare finally ended when I began to ask the right question. What am I doing to always attract the liars, cheaters, and deceivers? I began to look inward. I fasted, prayed, and set apart time to sit quietly and listen to God. I began to understand that what I thought about, I brought about. I saw myself as a victim, so I became one. I attracted men who looked for victims. I wore naiveté and gullible like a garment. I closed my eyes to the obvious. I did not make them earn the trust I had given them. Over and over, I let people lie to me without consequence, so it became easy for them. I was afraid that offending them would reflect poorly on who I am supposed to be in Christ. I cared too much about trying to impress others with my self-righteousness by proving I can forgive anything. I allowed them to take advantage of me by giving them too much power. And I gave away my security trying to be a people pleaser. Instead of letting Jesus be the Savior, I tried to represent Christ in a way He never intended. Christ demands a standard of living. He never intended for me to be a doormat and neither should you.

I chose this topic to focus on because I want women to know that who you choose to connect your life with can destroy your future, your hope, and derail your destiny. Who you seek out or attract is a true indication of how you feel about yourself and your self-worth. Jesus wanted me to come face to face with all my misses and messes. I had to ask God to show me how to get out of the horrible dreams. If my nightmare played over and over and over and the main character in every scene was me, then I was the problem. I was ignorant of the enemy's devices to get me to destroy my own hopes, dreams, and future. But even in all of this, Jesus still had a plan from the beginning. Jeremiah 29:11 says, "For I know the plans I have for you," declares the LORD, "plans to prosper you and not to harm you, plans to give you hope and a future" (NIV). The struggle was necessary to help me see what I was carrying around inside me. The fire of life had to get devastatingly hot to bring the deeply rooted issues to the surface. 1 Peter 4:12 says, "Beloved, do not be surprised at the fiery ordeal which is taking place to test you [that is, to test the quality of your faith], as though something strange or unusual were happening to you" (AMP). Joseph said it best in Genesis 50:20, "As for you, you meant evil against me, but God meant it for good in order to bring abou t this present result, to preserve many people alive" (NASB).

I stopped waiting for someone to give me what God already says I have. I stopped looking for permission to be great because I am already great. I raised the bar on my expectations of others. I connected with people who impressed me and saw value in me. I know that I am worthy to be among greatness, not pretentiousness. Because of walking in the light of truth, I am now fully awake. Jesus brought the most amazing man into my life who is nothing like any man I ever dated before. After six years of marriage, we are still honeymooning. We are truly evenly yoked, serving God as one unit. When I stopped looking, God presented me with my gift. God has done exceedingly and abundantly above all that I could ever ask or dream. I am living my dreams!

My company, N2Fruition, LLC, of Winston, Georgia, hosts an annual Women's Retreat in the North Georgia Mountains to address many struggles women face. They learn how they can successfully break through their cocoons and glide on their wings of deliverance. I became a Certified Master Personal Fitness Trainer offering boot camps in the community to help women love themselves inside and out. I also organize our Annual Christmas Cantata and Toy Giveaway through my church. We are celebrating six years of sharing the love of Christ and serving hundreds of children in the community with food, fellowship, and toys. I am Souled Out for Jesus!

My struggles were His strategy for my strength. I am a beautiful butterfly who embraced the struggle to fight my way through my cocoon, which was necessary to give me strong, lovely wings that carry me now. I am adorned with pearls created over years of encasing many irritants of life in the iridescent nacre of love. My eyes are like diamonds that could only have resulted from extreme pressure of the hardships I endured, but they sparkle with the joy of peace. And I have come forth as pure gold, tried in the immense heat of the refiner's fire; hot enough to burn off my impurities. My struggles were for good, to bring about the present result in me and to preserve many women alive for the kingdom.

Yield your mind, will, and emotions and get Souled Out for Jesus!

Surrender to Faith and Let God Do Your Heavy Lifting

CHERYL J. KETCHENS

"I want to be a woman who overcomes obstacles by tackling them in faith instead of tiptoeing around them in fear."

-Renee Swope

Have you ever been faced with a struggle or adversity so big it paralyzed you and left you feeling numb? Have you ever felt anxious, depressed, or overwhelmed? Maybe you're struggling to bond with your new baby and feeling like you won't survive?

I survived two very dark and challenging life struggles. One began on January 12, 1971, when a very anxious young woman in her early twenties went into labor and was about to give birth to her first baby. No more horror stories from other Moms about difficult pregnancies and nightmarish child births.

Two hours and twenty-one minutes after Michael and I made our frantic dash to the hospital, I gave birth to a beautiful, healthy, screaming, 7-pound, 8-ounce, 21-inch-long baby girl! Everything seemed great! Then, the first of two very difficult struggles began when the doctor informed us I had a serious infection and our baby had RH Factor, a very serious blood-borne illness that occurs when a mother is Rh- (dd) and her fetus is Rh+ (DD or Dd). Maternal antibodies had crossed the placenta and destroyed our baby's red blood cells. We had to find compatible blood donors immediately!

After a week-long nightmarish stay in the hospital and frantically trying to find compatible donors, we were released from the hospital with no transfusion needed! When the baby and I got home, I was ready to settle into a comfortable schedule and resume some normalcy in my life. But, roughly two weeks after dodging our life-threating RH crisis, struggle number two reared its ugly head. In many ways, it seemed far worse than the first.

At my daughter's first wellness check-up, I learned that she had colic. Between the horrific RH health scare, frantic calls to find compatible blood donors, and my post-birth infection, I was feeling overwhelmed, anxious, depressed, suicidal, and alone! I wasn't sure I could handle much more. Are you ready for struggle two?

Psychotic thoughts began seeping into my brain like a slow IV drip. My thoughts were surreal and certainly not based in reality. I knew my thoughts were wrong, completely irrational, and against my core values and beliefs; yet, I felt hopeless and lacked control. Have you ever felt powerless over your circumstances?

Weeks went by and I was still feeling like I did several weeks earlier, except for two uninvited monsters that showed up. They were the vicious kind—anger and rage! There were a few others as well, but these two were the worst among them. I felt like I was drowning at sea and no one was trying to save me. That's when the voices inside my head made their debut. Can a new Momma get a break? Have you ever felt alone and helpless? This was supposed to be a happy season in my life. Instead, I was filled with anger, rage, and suicidal thoughts.

During that period, I also harbored feelings of anger and rage toward Michael. He didn't seem to notice. The voices told me he was responsible for my madness and my world turning upside down. Why should he have a haven at work all day while I was living with pain and anguish? I wanted him to suffer like me. Having a baby right now was his idea not mine. I wanted to return to school and wait a while longer. My shyness, lack of self-confidence, and no plan shattered that dream. It would be many, many years later before I would tell him how I truly felt about having a baby when we did.

As my psychosis reached fever pitch, I was terrified to be left alone with my innocent little baby girl. She was one of God's greatest gifts; still, her incessant colicky cries tormented me, and I was angry and in rage. Her cries sounded like a large drum pounding against my cerebrum.

One afternoon, I put her down for her nap in her swing on our large enclosed porch. It was adjacent to our kitchen. She could nap, and I could keep an eye on her while doing my dishes. The sun was shining. It was the perfect place for her to nap. Literally moments after putting her into the swing, she woke up and started crying. At first, her cries were intermittent crackling ones then they escalated to full blown screams. I was exacerbated with her demands. For what seemed like an eternity, I stood in the kitchen doorway emotionless and numb. I clenched my teeth and clutched the doorframe as I watched and listened to her swing and scream, swing and scream. I refused to let her see me. Doesn't she realize her screams are making Mommy crazy? Does she even care how Mommy feels? Why won't she take her nap and leave Mommy alone?

Now that this precious little miracle was here, I resented her for disrupting my life. My time was no longer my own and I was angry about it. My psychosis was still gaining momentum by the day. The voices were telling me to step over the threshold separating the two rooms, grab the baby from her swing, and shake her delicate little body until I silenced her screams. Oh, my dear God! I was completely insane! Have you ever felt out of touch with reality?

During this very dark season in our lives, I didn't have a clue what was happening to me or if I would ever return to normalcy. It would be nearly three decades, two more babies, several job changes, and a couple of moves before I would learn what happened to me in 1971. Yes, I said two more babies! If you're wondering what happened there, those two pregnancies, births, and babies were great! Both boys were exceptional babies. Low maintenance, slept through the night, and napped during the day so Momma could too. Thank God!

On Wednesday, May 4, 2005, a young actress whom I'd fanaticized about meeting showed up in my living room during an episode of *The Oprah Winfrey Show*. It was the beautiful Brooke Shields. She was always one of my favorites.

I plopped down on the couch to watch. With tears welling up in her eyes, and a grave look on her face, Brooke recounted her story of suffering with postpartum depression (PPD). My heart raced a bit. I was mesmerized by her PPD struggles, the anguish and remorse she felt, and how she suffered in silence for fear of jeopardizing her career. Brooke's story was my story too. I wanted to jump through the TV screen, hug and kiss her, and thank her for sharing her story!

After nearly three decades, the mysterious post-birth psychosis was finally solved, and the beast's name: postpartum depression! Thank you, Brooke Shields, for sharing your story and helping me realize that I was not alone in the world. Possibly millions of women around the globe were also suffering in silence while harboring feelings of guilt and remorse for something outside of their control. The second of two horrific struggles was finally over!

During this very dark and tumultuous season in my life, I seldom stopped long enough to think rationally. When I finally did, I asked myself several questions.

1. How did I get to this place of insanity? My pregnancy was relatively easy, I had followed my doctor's orders, I had taken good care of myself, and my delivery went well.

2. Why do I feel so angry, depressed, suicidal, and emotionally detached from my new baby and my husband?

3. Where can I go for help and support? My husband has no clue, my beautiful mother is from the "Silent Generation" (they don't talk about anything related to sex), and I'm petrified to talk with my doctor!

4. Do you want to spend the rest of your natural life alone, isolated, and crazy?

These four simple questions were cathartic for me. I immediately began to feel more in control of my life. It was time to take the steps necessary to change my circumstances. I went from reactive to proactive.

During my season of postpartum depression, there were many, many pivotal moments that taught me valuable lessons about trusting God! My greatest pivotal moment occurred on the sunny afternoon that I put my baby into her swing to nap and she woke up. Remember the doorway of the kitchen where I stood emotionless, clenching my teeth, and gripping the doorframe, as I watched and listened to her swing and scream, swing and scream? Remember the voices that were telling me to step over the threshold, grab my baby from the swing, and silence her cries? In that moment, I knew I needed to trust God! I prayed like I never prayed before and called out to God to silence the voices inside my head. I can still hear His voice whispering in my ear as though it were yesterday. "I protected your mother many, many years ago, and I will protect you too my child. You must trust Me, believe in Me, rely on your faith, continue your prayers, and speak My name with pride to your neighbors."

"Never be afraid to trust an unknown future to a known God."

-Corrie ten Boom

Here are my Top Three New Mommy Action Steps, designed to educate and assist in the creation of a more positive new Mommy experience.

1. Read, Read, Read! Before your delivery, learn as much as you possibly can about post-baby changes that may occur psychologically and physiologically. Being proactive will help you have a more enjoyable birthing experience.

2. Know Your Family's Child Birthing and Medical History—Talk with your mom about her child birthing experience(s), your grandma, and any other close blood relatives who can share their experiences with you.

3. Create a New Mommy Support Team—The more support you have the better! This will keep you actively engaged with other Moms, both young as well as seasoned ones like Baby Boomers.

God, faith, and prayer were my support systems during my seasons of struggles. I literally prayed my way back from the depths of postpartum depression. The '70s were different than today! The elders believed solely in God, faith, and prayer for everything! Today, you have an abundance of resources and support systems available to you. Take advantage of them!

As a new Mom, it's natural to experience being overwhelmed, anxious, fatigued, and have many highs and lows. It's important that you remember you are not alone on your journey. Keep God first and everything else will fall into place.

Here is a great resource for Scripture and verse readings I recommend to new Moms:

The Bible Gateway Website. Learn more: www.bible-gateway.com

Here are a few Scripture and verse readings I like:

"Children are a gift from the LORD; they are a reward from him."

Psalm 127:3 (NLT)

"Start children off on the way they should go, and even when they are old they will not turn from it."

Proverbs 22:6 (NIV)

"The Lord is my strength and my shield; my heart trusts in him, and I am helped."

Psalm 28:7 (CSB)

My biggest breakthrough happened on the day I stood in the doorway of my kitchen watching and listening to my baby swing and scream, swing and scream, and I called out to God for help!

I prayed, cried, and pleaded like never before for Him to silence the insane, psychotic voices and to keep me from stepping over that threshold, grabbing my innocent little baby from her swing, and causing irrevocable harm.

I knew immediately that God had answered my prayers. Affirmation of the breakthrough came when my baby peacefully fell asleep and the voices inside my head were silenced. All thoughts of harming my baby and my husband, and committing suicide were gone! I felt an unbelievable peace wash over me.

If I were faced with this same situation today, I would ask myself several questions:

- ▸ What are the symptoms of postpartum depression?
- ▸ What is my mother's child birthing and medical family history?
- ▸ What resources and support systems are available to me?
- ▸ Where do I find a clinician who understands my medial needs and my specific psychosis?
- ▸ How soon should I seek help?

Today, if I were helping a friend with a similar problem, I would help her problem solve by creating real-life scenarios like the one below. I would advise her to keep her faith, trust God, and let Him do the heavy lifting for her!

Scenario:

You just met a young woman at work named Linda. She's eight months pregnant with her first child, she just lost her husband four weeks ago in a car accident, her mother passed away last year from cancer, she's never met her father, and she had to return to work because she needs the money to support herself and her new baby. She has no relatives or friends nearby to support her. How would you advise her?

Response:

As I reflect upon one of the darkest seasons of my life, I learned many invaluable lessons from those struggles: 1)

You're never alone. There are others dealing with similar struggles. 2) It's important to have good support systems. 3) Take time to do your introspective work. 4) Map out a plan or strategy to change your circumstances. 5) Faith and Prayer are two of your most valuable allies. 6) Never give up. Trust God to fight your greatest battles and do the heavy lifting for you!

God Worked It Out for My Good

JENNIFER MORRIS

"For I am persuaded, that neither death, nor life, nor angels, nor principalities, nor powers, nor things present, nor things to come, Nor height, nor depth, nor any other creature, shall be able to separate us from the love of God, which is in Christ Jesus our Lord."

I want to share with you how God brought me through one of the toughest seasons of my life—a season composed of loss, heartache, pain, and then restoration! The year was 2011 and it started out great. My home was peaceful, my children didn't give me any problems, and my job was great. I had absolutely nothing to complain about.

You see, I became aware of God's presence back in 1997. I decided to trust Him with my life and with the lives of my children. I was a single parent of two boys and one girl. My children were my life and I was theirs. All we had was each other.

I remember back in 1994 when my first husband decided to leave us for another woman, during the time that I was five months pregnant with my little girl. I remember seeing them pointing at me while laughing and calling me fat. That broke me down! Here was the man that I loved and dedicated my life to, talking about me like a dog with his new woman. I gave him all of me and this was how he chose to treat me. I just couldn't understand it. The pain was indescribable. I wouldn't wish that kind of pain on my worst enemy. I thought about killing myself because the pain was so bad and the only way to stop it was to die. I thought about my boys and the little one growing inside of me, and how it wouldn't be fair to my mom to leave my children for her to raise. My children are a real blessing from God because without them I would be dead! I made the right decision and God has been leading and guiding me through this thing called motherhood, a job that I am elated to do, ever since. Oh, by the way, I remarried in 2001.

Back to 2011. Things began to spiral out of control around June. The organization I worked for was bought out by another company; therefore, I lost my job. My son drowned at a lake in August just five days before he was scheduled to leave for Basic Training after joining the Air Force. My second husband walked out on me in January, five months after my son's death. A very close friend of mine died suddenly in March. My car, which my husband had stopped paying for, was repossessed in April. I remember thinking as the guy drove away in my car, "I can't take another thing, Lord! Please, make it stop!" I felt as though I was deflating, like all of the air was slowly seeping out of my body.

Despite of all of that, I still gave God the praise. I didn't understand what was going on, but I was a firm believer in Romans 8:28: "And we know that all things work together for good to them that love God, to them who are the called according to his purpose" (KJV). I knew that God's Word was true, and I believed that He was working it out for me because I truly love Him. I didn't have any money, my bills were due, and I didn't have any transportation—but God!

God opened the door for me to get my old job back. I was working with very awesome people. My office became the office of prayer because that is what I was known for. My coworkers would always commend me on how strong I was. What they didn't understand was that I possessed the peace God gives that passes all understanding, even mine. My relationship with God was vital. I had to stay focused on kingdom business to keep my mind off of my trials and tribulations. I took my role as a representative of the kingdom seriously. I could cry and scream in the midnight hour when it was just me and God, but when I stepped out of my house all anyone needed to see was the God in me; and God equals strength, grace, power, and above all, love!

God was sending people into my life just to help me financially. It seemed as though I was getting $500.00 checks written out to me from people I hardly knew, and the God thing was that I didn't even ask. Also, a member of my church let me keep her brand new F150 truck for as long as I needed it. I was blown away by her love and kindness. God really did that!

I didn't want for anything because God used others to meet my needs. I am so very grateful because I could have lost my mind, but God said, "Not so!" I really wasn't too surprised when my husband left because feelings on both of our parts had dissipated. I am grateful that God put it on his heart to make that move at that time because it really didn't hurt that much since I was still in the early grieving stages concerning the loss of my son. That pain superseded all other pains. God is so good!

One day at work, we were all sitting around waiting for a meeting to start. I heard one of my coworkers talk about dating sites. She had met several men on them. Out of curiosity, I decided to give it a try. I joined an online dating site called Christian Mingle during a July 4th special. It was very interesting to me because I had never done anything like that before. Immediately, I began receiving smiles from different men.

First, I need to share with you that I had a talk with God pertaining to the next man I would marry. And make no mistake, I meant marry. You see, I wasn't getting any younger and I didn't want to be anyone's girlfriend. I was ordained to be a Godly wife to a Godly husband, and I expressed that to God. I also made a vow to God that the next man that touched me in an intimate way would be my husband. The Bible says, "Death and life are in the power of the tongue" (Proverbs 18:21 KJV), and what I did was speak death over loneliness and life over love. I kept speaking it until it came to fruition. God's Word is true!

Anyway, by the end of July, I received a smile from this man named Richard Morris. He had four boys and his profile was very interesting to me. He was attractive. But most importantly, he loved God! That was the sexiest part of his profile. We talked on the site for a couple of months before we met. When we saw each other for the first time, there were no sparks at all; however, we decided to become friends. While that was happening, God was at work.

We talked on the phone every day, and he prayed for me before ending every call. He was very intentional about getting to know me. When I communicated with him the vow that I'd made to God, he was relieved because he felt the exact same way. He later told me that vow took away the pressure. As time went on, we grew closer. I finally met his boys and I knew what my role was going to be in their lives. On that following Valentine's Day, Richard asked me to marry him. We were married six months after we got engaged. We have been honeymooning ever since.

Out of my three marriages, this was the first one where I had something to look forward to. Yes, I'm talking about the honeymoon night. Leading up to it, there were some who said that I should try the sexual part of the relationship out before we got married; but, I am so thankful that I listened to God for guidance instead of people who have faith in their feelings. All of my faith is in God, and I was crazy enough to believe that He would make sure that everything was alright. I believe that because I made the conscious decision to wait and honor the vow that was made, my honeymoon and every moment since then has been magical. I know how to treat my blessing and he knows how to treat his.

I am now very proud to say that I am a housewife and a mother of eight beautiful children from the ages of 11-28. Our blended families get along great and we both look back over our lives and say, "Look what God has done." We recognize and give glory and honor to whom it is due and that is God Almighty. We trusted Him, and it paid off.

I encourage you to always look to God for guidance because He knows exactly what you need. He will never steer you wrong. I look back to where I was in 2011 in comparison to where I am now in 2017, and I can't help but to get emotional. I can't help but to praise Him. He is my Rock. He is my Provider. He is my Healer. He is my Restorer! He has brought me from a mighty long way—through so many storms, through so many valleys, and I still haven't lost my praise. I never thought that I would be in this position. I'm talking about a position of rest. Because of my obedience, because of my sacrifice, because of my belief, because of my faith, I can serve God from a position of rest.

The song that was sung at my wedding is called, "Bless the Broken Road." That was the perfect song for me and Richard because we didn't understand why we had to go down those roads. My husband lost his late wife of 23 years and he endured tremendous pain behind that loss. I lost my 18-year-old son and I endured tremendous pain. Those broken roads led us straight into each other's arms. Now, I'm here to help him and the boys deal with their loss and they are here to help me deal with mine. One line of the song says, "God blessed the broken road that led me straight to you." That song was the perfect choice for our special day.

It doesn't matter what you are facing, trust God and know that He is working everything out for your good. I'm a living witness, and I will share my testimony everywhere I go with whomever will listen. I cannot just sit down on the Good News of the Gospel of Christ. God has done way too much for me. Know who you are, know whose you are, and speak it. You are the righteousness of God. You are the apple of His eye. You are the head and not the tail. You are above and not beneath. You choose what you receive in your spirit and never allow anyone to take you out of your position.

I have been on this path for years. I'm talking about the path of righteousness. There are times when I become weak, but the Bible says, "My grace is sufficient for thee: for my strength is made perfect in weakness" (2 Corinthians 12:9 KJV). I have no room to judge anyone for anything because God has called us to love, not judge. My hope is that we can all be examples of the kingdom by showing the love of God to everyone, especially those who are not in covenant with God. Everyone needs to witness His love.

I encourage you to build on your relationship with God. Sometimes we are so focused on being loved down here on Earth that we neglect our relationship with God. Just remember that He is the One who loved us even when we didn't love ourselves. Know that He is the One that sticks closer than a brother. Know that He is the One that will never leave or forsake you. Those are the types of things you look for when building relationships. Take time to ask Him questions. Tell Him what's on your mind. Let Him know how you feel about Him.

Before I became aware of God's presence, I was looking for love in all the wrong places and in too many faces. But, when I realized what true agape love was, that is all I longed for. Jesus loved us so much that He gave His life for our sins so that we may have eternal life. Now that's love! I choose to live my life Souled Out for Christ. I feel like that's my reasonable service.

I really hope you were encouraged by my words and that you continue to look to Christ for your every need. Whatever you do, don't ever lose hope. Put your trust in God and He will make everything alright.

Forgiveness for the Brokenness of Daddy's Little Girl

LULA L. BOWENS

"Be strong and courageous. Do not be afraid or terrified because of them, for the LORD your God goes with you; he will never leave you nor forsake you."

Deuteronomy 31:6 (NIV)

As a little girl, your father is the most influential person in your life. We are often told that daddies are our first love. They set the stage for how you should be treated, protected, guided, and loved with proper and tender care. But, what happens when you wake up one day and Daddy decided to leave? What happens when you develop a hardened heart at age five? Well, I can tell you for me, I invited bitterness and hate in as my new best friends. I resisted hearing the truth about forgiveness for many years. I felt that I was justified in my reactions to his actions!

I blamed my father for all the bad things that happened to me. In fact, I buried a lot of my hurts and pains to avoid facing things. The only thing is, I didn't even know that I was doing it. I was literally a zombie walking around until my twenties. When my parents got their divorce, I was just entering pre-kindergarten. My father told me that even though my mother and he were not together, he would always be around if I needed him. He didn't keep that promise. That is when I first learned disappointment. I mean that type of disappointment that causes so many of us to struggle with forgiveness.

My mother had just started a new job. She didn't know how to drive yet. She arranged for a teacher at the elementary school where I would be attending to pick me up. He never bothered me because he had a boyfriend. There was a lady who lived directly across from the baseball field of the school. She would keep me for a few hours until he got off work. I didn't like my babysitter's neighbor because her brother lived with her. He was always looking at me. He was always talking about how pretty I was. He would always try to touch me or want to kiss me on my mouth.

One day, my babysitter left me with her neighbor. I went to the bathroom and when I opened the door her brother was standing outside of the door waiting for me! He said, "Now I got you." So, I took off running past him. He grabbed my arm, but I fought him and managed to get away. He almost had me back in the bathroom. That was the first time I was actually scared. I would call my father and leave him messages telling him about the bad man. He didn't call me back. I called him every day for weeks. Still, he didn't call me back.

After my father didn't call me back, my mom told me to stop calling him. She was trying not to tell me what would hurt me. I was persistent because my dad and I were close. Eventually, she told me that he said he didn't want anything to do with me. Something in me clicked and I just wasn't the same. I asked my mom if I could change schools. She said no, I couldn't just change schools for no reason.

Henry noticed the change in my behavior. He asked me one morning on the way to school. "What's wrong?" I didn't say anything. My teacher saw a change in me too. She called Henry away from his class and told him she believed I was being molested. He said, "I have been taking you to school every day and I see a change in you. I can't help you if you don't talk." He started asking probing questions. "Is it your dad? Is someone bothering you?" That's when I started crying. He asked me who and I told him about the bad man. He assured me he would take care of everything. He left his class when my day was over, and he met with my babysitter. He told her what was happening. Then, he asked her to take him to the bad man. In so many words, he told him he better not lay a hand on me or he would have to deal with him.

The babysitter would still leave me with the neighbor. The brother didn't care, and he still tried to get to me. One day, Henry didn't show up to pick me up for school. He was shot and killed over the weekend. My mom was able to transfer me to a school that was within walking distance from our house. Only trouble seemed to follow me. My new babysitter was great, and she had a son that I could play with and watch cartoons. Her father was always nice to me, but his wife was jealous. That is what he would say to me. He was too friendly. His wife would murmur derogatory statements and she tried to poison me twice. I would pray for God to help me, even at age five. My brother who is 16 years older than me was a preacher. I believed in God.

If you have had a very difficult childhood as it pertains to being protected, you are not alone. I developed a hard heart at a very young age. I can even be so bold as to say that in my ignorance I had a distrust of all men and some women. It was not very far off that I had a problem with authority; specifically, if they reminded me of dear old Dad. I viewed forgiveness like it was a tough fill-in-the-blank question on a test. So, if you don't know the answer, skip it! I skipped on forgiveness. I didn't want to date. My biggest fear was giving my heart to someone who would leave me just like my father. I ran off any and every man from ever getting close to me. I was a pro at how to lose a guy in 10 minutes or less.

In 2002, I switched departments at the local insurance carrier where I was working. We had to obtain our insurance license to become agents. There was this guy and we were respectful, but we really didn't associate with each other. Once we became licensed, we had the same supervisor and eventually we became best friends. I hadn't realized just how close I let him get to me. My guard was down with him.

The turning point for me was when my sister and I were talking one day. Out of the blue she said, "You know that you are one of the sweetest people that I know personally. One day, you will allow a man to see all you have to offer. You don't even see just how your father's absence has affected you. That's his problem because he missed out on knowing a great person." I started to ask myself some serious questions like: Am I really affected by my father's absence? Why do I really struggle with forgiving him? Am I going to be a bitter, old single lady with 90 cats? Why do I find fault in every man who shows an inkling of interest in me? Why don't I want to date? Will I ever recover? Can I love freely without fear?

One day, my coworker (the guy who worked his way into the friend zone) said to me in an email, "You can knock off the crazy act. I am not going anywhere." I was a little taken aback. I got up and walked over to his desk. I asked, "What do you mean I'm acting crazy?" He said, "I don't even think you realize that you do it. The closer we get, the more you cut up. You try to push me away. It probably works on other men. You are my friend and I love you, so I just ignore you. I'm not going anywhere, and you can't make me." That just meant the world to me. He actually meant every word. He said, "I think you need to find your dad and forgive him. I forgave mine, now it's your turn."

He offered to go with me to my father's house. I said, "No, I don't think showing up will be such a good idea." So, I decided to write him a letter. I wrote him two just in case the first one was not deliverable. I never received a response or phone call. I said a prayer and I gave it all over to God. You have to make a conscious decision to forgive, even when it is a tough situation. Even when the person who may have hurt or offended you is not around. I will be the first to admit that unforgiveness was taught to me by friends and family throughout the years. I didn't grow up in an environment where people were quick to forgive and release others of their actions. Sure, people spoke about forgiveness, but their actions never matched. It is the worst form of competition over the Word of God. In the church they call it the "flesh." We do what feels good over doing what's righteous.

Not long after I lost my job due to a departmental layoff in 2006. And I tell you, it was the best thing that ever happened to me. I wasn't going to church or reading my Bible as I should. Nothing draws you closer to God than being at the bottom. Being at the bottom is sometimes how God can get your attention. I felt like being at the bottom, God was able to put me in serious check. He loves us too much to let us self-destruct. We have to be smart enough to recognize when He is placing us in time out. It's not punishment! He's rebuilding us to be better.

It was during this time, that He worked on me with my problem of forgiveness for my father. Had I not been laid off work, I would not have been home during the day to channel surf and land on a sermon. The sermon was on forgiveness. I listened with great intent and before it was over I was on my knees asking for forgiveness. I was telling God I didn't want to be bitter and to please help me become a better person. I felt like such a huge weight had been lifted. It didn't stop there.

I stopped being a spoiled brat. Meaning I was blessed, but I didn't really appreciate all God had blessed me with until unemployment struck. I expected things although I never boasted. I just wasn't appreciative of it. I stopped praying idle talk. I stopped praying what I needed. God knows every-thing. I started showing more gratitude. I started each day only saying what I am grateful for that's in my life. Unless I was prompted to say an intercessory prayer for someone else, I would only say The Lord's Prayer and a separate gratitude prayer. That is when my life started to really turn around and blossom.

God blessed me with a job that I did not apply for at a world-renowned clinic. One morning, I was saying my gratitude prayers in the car. I was on my way to work. I heard an audible voice clearly say, "Death is coming, pray." To be honest, I was startled and confused. I wondered why I had heard what I did. That voice had such peace behind it. I definitely wasn't hallucinating. In fact, I used to side eye people who claimed that the Holy Spirit had spoken to them. I started praying for my mother because she did die the year before, but God gave her back. I went on to work.

The very next day, I was saying my gratitude prayers on my way to work, and the voice spoke again. This time He said, "Death is coming, pray for your father." If you could see the look on my face. I remember scrunching my face thinking, "My father?" I said, "Lord, I know that you don't have to answer me as you have already instructed me. I just need to know should I go see him?" He responded, "No, just send flowers." I said, "Okay." I said a prayer for my father. I asked God to please not hold against him how he treated me. I had forgiven him, and I would like very much for Him to wipe the slate clean as He says in His Word. I know that I was mad for a long time. None of that matters anymore. I have always loved him. In that very moment, I knew once and for all I had truly forgiven him.

A date kept popping up on all the floral websites, so I set that date as the delivery date. I sent him a bouquet of Birds of Paradise flowers. I told him in a note, "I love you, Daddy, even if you don't feel the same way." I left my phone number if he wanted to call me. I later learned that he passed after receiving my flowers. My note was missing and nowhere to be found. It is believed that he had it in his possession. I know that is true because the Lord spoke again. This time He said, "Your father loves you." He had to have seen my note!

Here is my takeaway. We often make judgments based upon what we see happening. We forget to consider other people's pain and circumstances that caused them to behave the way they do. God revealed some truth about my father. He didn't call me back, but he called the school, disenrolled me, and enrolled me in a new school. He just didn't bother to tell my mother. He had a rough childhood and he mimicked what he was taught. He remarried, and he never told his wife that he had a child. He said he didn't want anything to do with me, but he paid his child support.

I would encourage anyone who struggles with forgiveness to ask God for help. You need to know why you are really upset. It's not just one incident. One incident can be the source of other problems. It is masked differently depending on the person. Forgiveness of a person can literally create a healing manifestation in your life for other areas. Don't be so quick to ignore your own truth. Ask God to reveal all of the hidden areas in your life that are keeping you in bondage. Once He reveals it, tackle it! Conquer!

About the Authors

Karla Fuller

Karla Fuller's divine purpose is to encourage others. Raised in St. Louis, Missouri, in the A.M.E. Church, she earned BA/JD degrees from St. Louis University. She was the first African- American law clerk for the U.S. District Court, ED MO, and first woman/African-American, Regional Counsel, U.S. Nuclear Regulatory Commission.

Karla is involved with organizations such as: Leadership Texas Alumna, National Bar Association, National/ Texas State Association of Parliamentarians, and Sigma Gamma Rho Sorority, Inc. Her awards include: Mid-Cities Links Sallye Moore Award, Quaker Oats/NCNW Community Leader Award, Federal Executive Board Community Service Award, and Who's Who in Government Services.

Karla serves in the Greeter's Ministry at Oak Cliff Bible Fellowship, and enjoys being a part of their Couples4Life Small Group and Women of Transformation Prayer Group. She resides in Arlington, TX., where she is married to Byron Fuller, step-mother to Shayna and Sederick, and grandmother to Akil and Alahna.

Dr. Renee Fowler Hornbuckle

Dr. Renee Fowler Hornbuckle: author, businesswoman, motivational speaker, senior pastor, advocate, and life and crisis coach has always been drawn to helping others solve problems. Equipped with a passion for empowerment, she inspires others to transform their lives, reach their fullest potential, and get the corresponding results desired. Renee lived the "American Dream" with a successful marriage, thriving ministry, fruitful relationships, and lucrative businesses until 2005 when a scandal concerning her ex-husband changed their lives dramatically. Her family, congregation, and community were paralyzed; followed by shame, suffering, and sorrow along with the spiraling loss of finances, relationships, and possessions.

Left with the barebones of a shattered life and ministry, Renee found herself humiliated, embarrassed, stripped of all dignity, and left with unanswered questions. She along with her three children Matthew, Rachel, and Jordan (who she raised alone) chose to rise, declaring, "No matter what happens" they would make it through!

Learn more at www.ReneeHornbuckle.com

Robert Faulk

Robert Faulk is the founder and senior pastor of Faith Tabernacle World Outreach Center, Sumter, South Carolina. The church began with a Tuesday night Bible Study held at Ramada Inn on January 7, 1997. Pastor Faulk and his wife of 29 years, Pastor Kaldejia Faulk, are the proud parents of three children—David, Deborwah, and Nehemiah.

Pastor Faulk's vision for Faith is "to increase God's family with people transformed by His word, showing compassion to Christ's body, and outreach to the world as we glorify God through worship." Pastor Faulk reaches communities and people throughout Sumter by teaching the Word of God with simplicity.

In addition to his ministerial duties, Pastor Faulk has goals to foster unity among the races, fellowship among churches, and rebuild the wastelands in Sumter and surrounding counties.

Pastor Faulk is a member of Destiny Life Ministries International (DLMI) and the Association of Independent Ministries (AIM).

Learn more at www.faithtabernaclesc.org

Shani McIlwain

Hilarious and transparent are two words that describe Shani as a speaker. Known for her candid personal stories, she weaves her "messy" moments of life into practical teaching moments for others. Shani McIlwain is the host of her own BlogTalk radio show that airs every Monday night where she shares love, light, and life with thousands of listeners across the country.

Shani motivates her audiences with practical principles for being effective in all areas of life. Her transformative messages help people change their mindsets, shift perspectives, and maximize the potential within.

Shani is the author of two bestselling devotionals, *Sharing My Mess: 90 Days of Prayer and Spiritual Intimacy with God* and *It's Time to Make a Change: 30 Days to Renew Your Mind, Heart and Soul*. Using prayer as a catalyst for change, Shani teaches audiences how to apply prayer habits into daily practices.

Learn more at www.sharingwithshani.com

Cynthia Fox Everett

Cynthia Fox Everett is a mother of four and a grandmother of seven. A U.S Army veteran of 14 years, Cynthia also has an Associate's Degree in Criminal Justice/Protective Services and furthered her education at Shaw University.

Cynthia rededicated her life to Christ in 2003, and accepted the mission and the responsibility to serve in the house of the Lord. She is driven to make a tangible difference in the lives of others, including her fellow veterans.

Cynthia's mission is to inspire and empower others to seek Jesus for the strength to heal so that they will have the courage to rewrite their future, tell their story, and help others heal. She strives to love unconditionally and to teach others how to love themselves, so that they feel and know genuine love for a lifetime.

To connect, email her at invisibletovisible2017@gmail.com

Nicole Matthews

Currently residing in Florida, Nicole Mathews is an author, a certified peer recovery specialist, a happiness coach, and a motivational speaker who specializes in happiness and positivity. She has energy, a solid record of accomplishment, and an extensive involvement in her field of skill. She believes in utilizing her impeccable encouragement and interpersonal skills to help and guide people, mostly women, in overcoming all obstacles and to ensure they always become their best selves while living a happier life.

After spending over 20 years in Corporate America, Nicole noticed the many distractions that keep people from living happier lives and reaching their full potential. She realized that the corporate world has pitfalls that can hinder experiencing true joy. This experience influenced her decision to launch her two businesses: Departing Depression and Happy Soul Habits.

Nicole is the mother of two children and the grandmother of three grandsons.

To connect, email her at nicolegmatthews@gmail.com

Silvester Lewis Jr.

Silvester Lewis Jr., is a self-described people person with a passion to make people laugh and see the positive side of life. Retired from Kaiser Hospital after 18 years of dedicated service, Silvester is an avid sports fan. He also loves bowling and playing checkers, dominoes, and pool.

Silvester attends Liberty Church in Fairfield, CA. He has two children, eight grandchildren, and three great-grandchildren.

Catherine Davis Wright

Catherine Davis Wright, born and raised in Savannah, Georgia, has been destined for greatness. She is married to William Wright and has an exceptional seven-year-old daughter, Cayden Kennedi. She believes it is vital to trust God with everything.

Catherine has a Master in Business Administration and works in the healthcare industry. She believes that it is important to bring great people and organizations together. Catherine is working toward becoming an entrepreneur and giving back to the community. She manages her daughter and husband and actively works with youth.

To connect, email her at cdavis1563@icloud.com

Betty Speaks

The Extraordinaire Betty Speaks "IT!" is an award-winning, certified master storyteller, with a focus on intentional transformation. She honorably retired from the U.S. Army, and is a global network virtual marketer/entrepreneur, a two-time bestselling author, and an ordained pastor.

Betty holds a Bachelor's in Business Law from the University of Maryland, College Park, Maryland. She received three "Outstanding Businesswoman of The Year" awards from the American Business Women's Association.

Betty's mission is to assist and guide individuals and couples through their personal and professional challenges, providing faith-based mentorship to design an individualized plan that will propel them into their God-given purpose!

Betty brings to value over 20 years of military experience, over 10 years in multiple avenues of ministry, and 24 years of marriage and raising a blended family. Her extensive educational background and experience affords her the tools to intentionally transform your life.

Learn more at www.Bettyspeaks.com

Denise Polote-Kelly

Denise Polote-Kelly is the owner of D. Kelly Management, an encourager, and a life transformation coach. She is a sought-after speaker and an award-winning, #1 multiple best-selling author. Denise is also a Grief Recovery Specialist.

Denise serves as an Imerman Angels Mentor for cancer patients, caregivers, and survivors. She has appeared on WTOC, WSAV, and throughout the South East and the Bahamas. She has been featured in the Huffington Post, CovNews, Savannah Tribune, and Herald of Savannah. She has also been a feature at the Southern Women's Show. Denise is a President's Club member of the Christian Women in Media Association (CWIMA), TLOD, Inc., and the NAPW. She founded the Winston H. Kelly, Sr. Memorial Foundation and Laps for Life. Her book helped to fund research, provide education about stomach cancer, and assist families.

Learn more at www.denisepolotekelly.com

Donna Davis-Curry

Donna Davis-Curry, wife of Reginald L. Curry Sr., has a well-blended-family with children: Reginald Jr., Asia, Sasha, Catherine, and Chynna, and grandchildren: Shania, Cayden Kennedi, Shayla, and Reginald, III. Her motto is, "I can only be me."

Donna is an ordained minister, founder of Intimate Circle Ministries, Incorporated, and co-founder of God's Anointed People Ministries (GAP). She is a sought-after speaker, philanthropist, community leader, and teacher of God's Word. She is the coauthor of the Amazon #1 bestseller, *Soul Talk*, with Cheryl Polote-Williamson as the visionary.

Donna has initiated many conferences such as:
* Divine Woman Within: Where is She?
* Spiritual Spa: Detox and Spiritual Makeover
* Alabaster Box: What is your Gift?
* Circle of Love
* Removing the Mask
* The Cultivating Experience—A New Budding

Her ultimate goals are to build a community shelter to house the homeless and to create a resource center.

Learn more at intimatecircleministriesinc.org

Kaldejia Faulk

Kaldejia Faulk, known affectionately as Lady Dee Faulk, is an associate pastor, author, purpose coach, and inspirational speaker. She currently holds an Honorary Graduate Degree in Social Work from HBCU Benedict College in Columbia, South Carolina.

Kaldejia's greatest achievement, following being a wife, mother, and grandmother, is impacting the lives of men and women who are in transition from doing life to embracing purpose.

As a conqueror of depression, and overcomer of negative self-talk and emotional trauma, she has embraced her purpose assignment: to empower men and women to embrace God's purpose for their lives and impact the masses.

Learn more at www.faithtabernaclesc.org

Shirley Jean Bazemore

Shirley Jean Bazemore is a motivational speaker residing in Greenville, North Carolina. She is a graduate of Elizabeth City State University with a BS in Criminal Justice from Elizabeth City, North Carolina. A retiree from East Carolina University with 30 years of experience as a Parking Enforcement Supervisor with East Carolina University, Shirley was awarded the Business Services Quest for Excellence Award for Outstanding Supervisor, East Carolina University Chancellor's Synergy Award for Team Work, the Pirate Wellness Challenge for Your Well-Being, and the Outstanding Employee Performance Award. Shirley also served as the Staff Senate with the Chancellor's Office.

Shirley's professional training included: East Carolina University Certificate in Leadership, International Parking Institute Certificate, Rockhurst University Management Course, Rockhurst University Leadership and Supervisory Skills for Women, Supervision Institute Training Program, and International Parking Institute for Customer Service.

Shirley believes you should find your passion, purpose and plan in life, and pursue it.

To connect, email her at proverbsw17@gmail.com

Dr. Helena V. Hill

Dr. Helena V. Hill is the wife of Pastor Derrick Hill and the mother of a daughter, Quaneshia, and two sons, Shamar and D'Allen. She is a senior pastor, award-winning author, certified life coach/Christian counselor, and she holds a Doctorate of Divinity Degree.

Dr. Helena has served for over 30 years in numerous areas of ministry and pioneered several church organizations; two churches in the states, five church partnerships in Trinidad, and her ministry in Pakistan. She has traveled to several cities and states as a seminarian and a speaker for radio, television, conferences, and organizations. Many have been healed from sicknesses and diseases under the mantel God has placed upon her.

As a life coach for the Fayetteville Housing Authority, Dr. Helena's seminars are credit hours applied toward the attending residents' housing. She hosts a monthly faith-based network social that brings awareness to the community of local businesses.

Learn more at www.teatimeletstalkblends.com

Cynde Joy

Cynde Joy has been working in the public school system for over 23 years. She is a certified special education teacher working as an autism specialist, a personal care attendant managing specialist, and on the behavior intervention team district wide. Her Bachelor's Degree is in Social Work and she has a Master's Degree in Education with Graduate Certificates in Autism Intervention and Behavior Analysis. She also has a treatment level foster home in her home for traumatized children.

Cynde has raised five biological children, two stepchildren, and adopted one child so far. She has many foster children that have lived in her home, and is a grandmother to 14 precious grandchildren.

Cynde has been on a spiritual journey following Christ for over 30 years. She is a member of the admin board at her church, Hope Community Church of the Nazarene. She is an experienced public speaker.

To connect, email her at Cyndejoy@yahoo.com

Robin Hair

Robin Hair is a passionate inspirational speaker and entrepreneur. She has a powerful story of an epic journey through many valleys meant to take her spirit, life, and soul. Her story evokes sorrow and pain, but also resilience, hope, renewal, and recovery through unwavering faith in God and His promises. "My struggles were for good, to bring about the present result in me and to preserve many women alive for the kingdom."

A graduate of Savannah State University, Robin Hair is a leader at Christ Apostolic Life Church, and holds a Master's degree in Business Administration.

Robin's company, N2Fruition, LLC, of Winston, Georgia, hosts an annual Women's Retreat in the North Georgia Mountains. Robin is a Certified Master Personal Fitness Trainer offering boot camps in the community. She is celebrating the launch of her 7th Annual Christmas Cantata and Toy Giveaway, serving hundreds of children, through her church.

Learn more at http://robinhairn2fruition.vpweb.com/

Cheryl J. Ketchens

Cheryl J. Ketchens is an entrepreneur, motivational speaker, coach, bestselling author of *Shift Happens*, a member of the National Women's Speakers Association, and a graduate of Spring Arbor University with a BA in Management and Organizational Development. As the CEO of Wellness Is Power, LLC, Cheryl's mission is to help new moms transition into parenthood after postpartum depression. She has received national certifications in Workforce Development and Toastmasters International "Advanced Communications and Leadership" Awards. Cheryl has also served as the 2016/2017 Mid-Michigan Area Director, 2016/2017 motivational speaker at Jackson College, and Keynote Speaker at the National Society of Black Engineers Corporate Staff Development Event.

Helping others achieve financial success and spiritual freedom is Cheryl's passion. She motivates and inspire audiences to take action.

Learn more at www.GreatnessOpensDoors.com

Jennifer Morris

Jennifer Morris was born and raised in the small town of Rolling Fork, Mississippi. She now resides in Oklahoma City, Oklahoma, with her amazing husband, Richard Morris, and four of their eight children.

Jennifer Morris is an amazing writer who loves to share her life experiences to help others. She has made it through many obstacles and believes that everything that she has gone through was for the sole purpose of helping someone else. In her first book, *Third Time Was the Charm*, written under the pen name LaTruth Fennell, she underlined her experience of finding true love after two failed marriages.

Jennifer is a woman after God's own heart and a prayer warrior in her own right. She loves God and His people. She is an ordained minister who loves to share the Good News of the Gospel of Jesus Christ.

To connect, email her at jenniferburnett2@aol.com

Lula L. Bowens

Lula Bowens has been in the financial industry for 21 years. During this time, she obtained her Health, Life and Variable Annuities License. She has a heart for people and loves to help anyone with her power. Her passions led her to her current position with a world-renowned clinic where she continues to work in the financial industry.

Besides working in the financial industry, Lula has a blog coming out to address virginity and abstinence in today's society. It is her desire to mentor the younger generations on virginity and abstinence, and empower them to make better choices.

To connect, email her at ThePursuitofPurity@outlook.com

Cheryl Polote-Williamson

Nationally acclaimed bestselling author, transformational speaker, and success coach Cheryl Polote-Williamson has established multiple platforms, dedicating her consulting practice to cultivate innovative business solutions, strategic marketing initiatives, and financial acumen for entrepreneurs. A global leader, Cheryl is the CEO and founder of Williamson Media Group, LLC, and Cheryl Polote-Williamson, LLC, where her knowledge and expertise is used as a conduit to affirm others in pursuit of their purpose.

Cheryl's unmatched credibility in the industry has earned her numerous awards, including the Chocolate Social Award for best online community, the Dallas Top 25 Award, and the Female Success Factor Award. She has been named among the Who's Who In Black Dallas Publishing, held a position on the Forbes Coaches Council, and participates in the NAACP Author Pavilion, the Congressional Black Caucus, Christian Women in Media, and the National Association of Women Business Owners.

A prolific author and winner of the 2017 Indie Author Legacy Awards, Cheryl has published multiple books, including *Soul Reborn, Words from the Spirit for the*

289 Spirit, Safe House, Affirmed, Soul Talk, Soul Bearer, and *Soul Source,* with more titles on the way. She is also producing a play entitled *Soul Purpose,* set for a 2018 debut.

Cheryl and her husband, Russell, currently reside in Flower Mound, Texas. They have three beautiful children, Russell Jr., Lauren, and Courtney, as well as an adorable granddaughter, Leah. In her spare time, Cheryl enjoys traveling, reading, serving others, and spending quality time with family and friends.

To learn more, visit her website at
www.cherylpwilliamson.com

Sources